**Praise For
Courage To Be Naked**

"Fred has spoken for my staff a few times. Every time, with great feedback. We are excited to share his new book with our staff members. If you are in a position where you need to communicate your message to others, I highly recommend reading this book and bringing Fred into your organization to speak."

**George De La Rosa - CEO
Toronto Star Credit Union**

"Fred Sarkari has been speaking within our industry for many years. As Canada's largest mortgage Company, with annual originations exceeding 10 billion dollars, we recognize the need for exceptional trainers and leading experts within our field. Fred, is one of the best on the planet. He is passionate, dynamic, and his messages are inspiring to all. I can't wait to get a copy of Fred's new book and we plan on distributing it to our 2000 agents Nationwide!! It will no doubt be ROCKET FUEL for our team!"

**Gary Mauris
Dominion Lending - Owner / President**

"I have been speaking professionally for over 10 years. This book will forever change the impact of your presentations. By far the best presentation book I have ever experienced in my career as a speaker."

**Andrea Thatcher - Pro Trainer,
Canfit Pro**

"We have all sat into Fred's sessions and his messages are inspiring and motivating. I enjoy reading and re-reading his books as I am always learning something new that I can immediately apply to my business and personal life. His ideas are incredible and I highly recommend both Fred's books as well as attending."

Tamara Stone – Remax
Contender for Real Estate Reality Show

"As a past professor, consultant and speaker, I was extremely impressed with Fred's speaking style. He has the unique ability to engage the audience, share relevant content and help the audience create an implementation plan. My staff has attended Fred's seminars and I am very excited for all of them to have this book. This book is a must read for anyone communicating a message."

Sandy Pembroke - 2005 World Kickboxing Champion
Owner, Your Gym Bag

"I met Fred while transitioning my engineering career. Doing coaching with him changed how I looked at my relationships in my professional and personal life. Participating in Fred's coaching and workshops, I regained my focus and direction. I have attended many of his sessions and was so excited to read this book. In my role as manager and professional engineer, I have to communicate with many different people in a fast paced environment. This book made a great impact in how I communicate my message on a daily basis."

Deanne Collinson, P.Eng - Civil Engineering Manager
Caltech Senex Oil & Gas group

"Fred has worked with my team on numerous occasions. We've had such great feedback everytime. Fred has played a significant role towards the 100% employee satisfaction results we achieved for 2010. This result is unprecedented for the software industry. We are so excited to get Fred's new book in the hands of our team members and look forward to working with Fred in 2011."

Jo Chubb- General Manager
L4U Library Software

"The lawyers and staff in my office have attended Fred's seminars. We all loved them. I strongly recommend making the time to read Fred's book and attending his seminars - You will be entertained and enriched."

Richard Montgomery, Lawyer
Montgomery and Miles Law Firm

" Fred Sarkari is a fantastic teacher and trainer. We have worked with Fred for a number of years and find him to be a great resource for maintaining clarity and business focus. We appreciate Fred's continued assistance in our dynamic and ever changing environment. All of our team are excited to receive his new book. This book is a must read for anyone who does presentations or training of any kind."

Rob Regan-Pollock, Broker-Owner
Invis

"I have been doing sales presentations for many years. The secrets in this book has not only changed the effectiveness of my message to my audience, but more so leave behind a lasting connection."

Sarah deBoer - MAS - A.T. Cross

"Fred Sarkari is truly one of the great communicators of his time. While on the surface it may seem as though his abilities are born out of natural skill and talent, the reality is that Fred has worked hard to perfect the art of story telling. His skills are learned and subsequently can be taught, and are skills that he will teach you through the Courage to Be Naked."
Nolan Matthias - Best-Selling Author of Forget Your Mortgage & Golf Balls Don't Float

"We have known Fred Sarkari as a friend and a mentor. His greatest gift is his sincerity, his passion and his ability to help others.
We all want happy productive employees. Fred has the uncanny ability to reach and touch each participant through his seminars and his books as if he was coaching them one on one.
I am a student of his powerful, inspirational and results oriented one on one coaching programs. The last couple of years have proven that only the strong survive. Let Fred show you and your company how to thrive in the coming years! – This is a must read book."
Cal DeSouza, CEO Belleview Communities

"This book will change how you communicate your message, whether to an individual or a group of thousands. This book consists of secrets of successful presenters and reading it will give you principles and tools to become a successful communicator on stage."

James Malinchak – Featured on ABC's TV Show, "Secret Millionaire"
America's Top Big Money Speaker Trainer
Founder of www.Bigmoneyspeaker.com

Courage To Be Naked

The Ultimate Guide To

Presenting And Communicating Your Message

From the best selling author
How The Top 5% Think!

"Present with the passion of a child and your audience will be transported from their seats to the playground."

Fred Sarkari

Library and Archives Canada Cataloguing in Publication

Sarkari, Fred
  Courage to be naked : ultimate guide to presenting
and communicating your message / Fred Sarkari.

Issued also in CD and electronic formats.
ISBN 978-0-9738108-4-4

  1. Public speaking. I. Title.

PN4129.15.S26 2011   808.5'1   C2011-900473-9

Contents

DEDICATED TO MY TWO ANGELS

The truth is I did not have to think twice before deciding how this book was to be dedicated. Two very special people in this world have been my inspiration and have taught me many things about business, life, relationships, love, compassion and fun. They have also taught me much about one of the most valuable life lessons - *the importance of being authentic.* As a result, I have learned more about myself than I ever thought possible.

I began writing this book many years ago as a guide to presentation skills to help others in their careers and provide them with tools to be more dynamic and successful.

Although I could never quite place my finger on it, I always felt that there was something missing and the book was somehow incomplete. I decided to hold off on finishing the book until I found the missing piece of the puzzle.

One day I was at a social gathering with my family. More than one hundred of us had gathered, enjoying food and drinks, mingling over clanging glassware and chattering. Suddenly the room fell silent. I looked over to see my niece and nephew, Natasha and Zal, on stage. As soon as they started speaking, the entire room was captivated. These two precocious children captured and held the attention of a room full of adults who listened to them intently, laughing and agreeing – Why were they all fully engaged?

That got me thinking about what these two children, 8 and 10 years of age, could have done to make an entire room of rowdy adults stop what they were doing and give them their full and undivided attention. Was it the funny things they said; the power of their voices; or the topics they were talking about?

The answer I was looking for appeared like a ray of light through the clouds. I knew exactly what was missing in my book. The missing piece of my puzzle had revealed itself through my niece and nephew.

Natasha and Zal were able to tap into their authenticity and were not fearful of being true to who they were – something that comes so naturally to children.

Both of these wonderful young people had their distinct style and they were authentic to it as they shared their message. There was no doubt in anyone's mind that these two were speaking from their hearts. They had not come with a memorized and polished speech - they were simply being authentic, and in turn, they were able to share, connect and touch the hearts of all those present. To this day, those privileged to have been in that room still talk about that moment. They cannot remember the exact words they heard, but they do remember how they felt.

I truly believe that to be successful in this world as a presenter, business owner, or even more so, as an individual, we need to be more authentic as a person.

As Natasha and Zal went on with their presentation that day, a second lesson became apparent to me. It was obvious to me and everyone else in the room that they were up there to have fun and they were thoroughly enjoying every moment.

In business, we too often see presenters who are so intent on getting systems to deliver their message in place that they forget the most critical element – to have fun along the way.

We create magic when we learn to enjoy the opportunity to share and connect with the audience instead of just trying to teach them something. When you have fun, your audience will have fun and, when they have fun... they learn.

As you can see, without the guidance I receive from Natasha and Zal, this would have been just another typical book on presentations and there would have been no life within these pages to share with you.

Natasha and Zal, the two brightest lights in my life, have reminded me that we as speakers should never lose sight of two very critical elements. First, be authentic; always be true to who you are and ensure that both your message and your delivery are heartfelt. Second, always remember to have fun along the way.

Acknowledgments

This book could not have been possible without the unparalleled support I have received from speakers throughout the years. Thank you so much for your invaluable guidance. Your insights and secrets have not only changed my career, but have made this book so much richer.

I would also like to extend thanks to all of the people who have supported me in my public speaking career. There is nothing more gratifying for me than hearing stories about the impact my presentations have had on your lives, and I truly appreciate everyone who has taken the time to share those stories with me. This type of feedback always reminds me why I do what I do and continues to drive.

Thanks also to all my friends and family, who have been unfailingly supportive of all my pursuits. Your consistent encouragement and palpable excitement has kept me going at all times. Your belief that I should write this book has been a critical motivating factor in moving it from a concept all the way through to publication.

To Lynda Norman, thank you for lending your skills not only to edit this book, but to remind me how important it is to surround yourself with good-hearted people.

Most importantly, I want to thank those who have donated to my cause for creating more camps for children - something that is important to me. To further my efforts to support this, I made the decision to give away my books for the first few months of publication and encouraged readers to donate instead. For those who followed through, words cannot describe my thanks.

Meaning of Courage

While this book is geared toward individuals who wish to improve their public speaking skills, the heart of this book is really much more than that. The Courage To Be Naked not only helps you onstage, but helps you live a fuller and more vibrant life overall. After all, that is what real courage is: whole-hearted people living their worthiness.

In fact, the word courage itself comes from the Latin word "cor," which means heart. People who have real courage are those who are willing to open themselves up and reveal their heart – their true self. They are willing to be imperfect and let go of who they think they should be in order to become who they are truly meant to be. People with real courage are essentially vulnerable; accepting that what makes them vulnerable is actually, what makes them beautiful, unique and special.

This type of courage seems like it comes naturally to some people. They are ready to shed their skin and just open themselves up to the world. For others, however, letting go of inhibitions and doubts is much more of a struggle.

For me, I have fought with this my entire life. Being vulnerable and exposed has never been second nature for me, even though I have always known deep within my soul that I wanted to be like that. Therefore, despite my developed inhibitions, I have spent many years surrounding myself with people who do possess such courage.

14

These individuals are often regarded as odd. Mainstream culture does not always understand or embrace the powerful quirks that these individuals willingly let shine. It is their desire to be who they are that makes them different. There is nothing more refreshing than meeting someone that posses true courage within them: courage to be themselves, no matter what.

I have seen no better example than in my niece and nephew. Children have the gift of honesty, plainly showing their feelings to the world. When they hurt, they tell you. When they love, they show you. My relationship with Natasha and Zal has been an important awakening for me.

By being around these people, I have discovered that courage is not simply something you are born with. It is something you cultivate. It has taken me years to let go of my fears and I have fought with myself countless times as I try to leave my skin by the door. It's literally been a street fight, of which I have lost some and won others. Over time, I've found my courage.

It is that courage that I want to share with you. It may not be easy, at times it may seem like a lonely road and it probably won't be comfortable, but ultimately, it's worth it.

Why the Title
"Courage To Be Naked" ?

When delivering a presentation I tell people to be authentic on stage, be the real you, stop being someone you are not and share from the heart. I am in essence, saying the only way to do that is to strip away that protective shell - be vulnerable, trust your inner voice... and be naked, exposing your heart and your message.

If presenters were to tap into the joy of why they do what they do, and have more fun with it, they would all be well on their way to being among the greatest speakers who ever walked on stage. In short, strip away the armor and have fun with whatever you do.

"Courage To Be Naked" will undoubtedly teach you the skills and psychology you need to be a proficient, effective and impactful speaker - a speaker who will leave a lasting impression in the hearts of any audience.

More importantly though, I know this book will inspire you to strip away your shell in order to be an authentic speaker and communicator.

Michelangelo's Greatest Gift –
Be Authentic

When communicating your message, whether you are addressing three people or an audience of thousands, you want to leave a lasting impression. You will truly reach your audience if you are clear about your purpose for being there, know the impact you want to make in their lives and are sincere about the connections you want to create. Most importantly, the more you are able to share your authentic self, the more likely it is that your presentation will live on in the hearts of your audience. To be able to connect fully with your audience you must embrace certain aspects of authenticity.

You can be the most powerful, interesting and captivating personality but if your audience is not open to receiving from you, none of that matters. In order for the audience to become open to receiving you must establish trust. If you expect your audience to be open to you and trust you, you need to be open and trust your audience.

"The only way you can achieve that mutual trust is by being authentic – most will see through the façade if you attempt to be someone you are not."

For most of us, trusting a group of strangers when we are in a vulnerable situation would seem impossible. So it is important to remember that when you

17

are open and trusting others will feel safe to trust you. When you establish that trust, the minds and hearts of your listeners will be open to receive your message.

Being authentic is also connected to truly caring about your audience - not judging them for how you see them or for how they respond or react, but truly caring about them.

Before you can truly care about someone, you have to be open-minded and listen to one another without judgment.

The most effective way of listening to your audience is to practice mindfulness – this is where you have complete awareness of your surroundings and those around you. There is a big difference between being mindful and concentrating. To be truly mindful means that you will never hold judgment of those around you.

Michelangelo, as we all know, is one of history's great creative geniuses.
In his time, speaking your mind usually resulted in imprisonment or death. How ironic, that in our time, what all people crave from others is that they speak their truth and are authentic.

In addition to his art, Michelangelo wrapped his vast mind around the great moral issue of all time: "How can we live a good and meaningful life?" He believed that finding inner peace was the key to creating a masterpiece that would live throughout history in the hearts of all.

To find inner peace is to know your values, understand why you are doing what you are doing and be true to it at all times.

In short, the authenticity Michelangelo applied to his life and his work is the reason his creations have remained forever cherished through the ages.

There is true power in having the courage to be authentic to our values, to who we are and what we are trying to create, whenever we have the opportunity to share a message to an audience of any kind.

Michelangelo sculpted *David* out of a "ruined" block of marble rejected by others. He said the statue already existed within that stone - he just needed to chip away the stone that hid the beauty of the statue.

As you read this, you will gain a deep sense of understanding about what it takes to shine on that stage and, if you are willing to chip away at the shell and have the courage to reveal your authentic self, you will in your own unique way, leave a masterpiece in the hearts of your audience.

Introduction

I f you are reading this book, you are probably looking for a way to improve your public speaking skills. The ideas and skills presented in this book however, apply to a wide range of situations. After reading this book, you will be equipped with principles to help you communicate better in all aspects of your life. You will find yourself relying on these ideas during one-on-one conversations with your employees, colleagues, friends, and family. Passages from this book will come to mind when dealing with your family or your friends. The insights from the following chapters will even help you when trying to write a book or a professional article. You will even discover that the principles explored in these pages can transform your business partnerships and help you accrue new clients. Ultimately, you can apply the sound communication skills offered in this book in both your professional and personal life.

As with any successful communication, when you are delivering a presentation, you should keep two variables in mind:

- What is your message?
- Does your message relate to your audience?

The goal of every presenter should always be to communicate information in a way that connects with his or her audience. Your presentation should engage your audience verbally and visually, and most importantly, emotionally. You want to deliver messages that not only excite the mind but also touch the heart, leaving an impression that lasts long after your presentation is over.

Presenters should never lose sight of these two critical aspects:

1. **The best way for an audience to learn is to connect your message to an emotion.**
2. **People will always remember how you make them feel.**

This book will cover the principles required to develop and deliver presentations and communicate a message that will successfully engage your audience. Your purpose in any presentation is to captivate your audience and stay true to your own philosophies and ideas, and we will outline how to accomplish this.

Every book on presentations inevitably includes a section that outlines what you should never do. The main thing to keep in mind throughout this manual and course is that there is no such thing as 'never'. Everything can serve as a guideline. You should not paint everyone with the same brush and the same applies to presentation styles – they are as individual as you are. If a specific style works for you on stage, then build on it.

We will cover guidelines and strategies that will help you to shape meaningful presentations and deliver them with powerful impact. You will also learn how to come across as a polished, confident, influential speaker who will leave a lasting impression within their minds and hearts.

Strong presentation and public speaking skills are essential. As a great communicator you will be effective at getting your point across to any audience – an invaluable skill in both professional and personal spheres.

There is power in developing the ability to entertain an audience. Entertainment is an influential factor in persuading people to listen to you, and more importantly, creating a lasting impact, in helping your audience tap into their own potential.

Anyone can become a powerful presenter if they understand the key components of successful presentations and know how to implement them based on their individual style.

"They must feel that you genuinely care about them."

Building Your Presentation

*"If I had only sixty seconds on the stage,
what would I absolutely have to say to get my
message across?"*

Jeff Dewar

The Invisible Man In The Hallway

"People do not care how much you know,
until they know how much you care."

One of my proudest moments happened when I was teaching College. One of my classes was a graduating class of business students who were ready to face the real world.

One day, I held an open discussion on what it takes to succeed in the business world. As we talked about the technical skills needed, understanding the financials of a company, marketing and sales it occurred to me that as educators, we at times are also missing what are in fact the real priorities in life and business.

I decided to give them a short quiz. One of the questions was; "What is the first name of the man who cleans the hallways at the college each day?

Most thought it was a joke. They had all seen this man countless times – they had passed by him every day they had attended college, yet most could not describe him or even pick him out of a line up.

As I expected, when I reviewed the answers, the list included almost every name you can imagine. Of course, everyone was hoping to guess the right name.

Finally one student asked the question I was waiting for - "Does that question count in any way towards our grade?"

My answer to the class was "absolutely not -but it does count in your career, the impact you will make and the kind of leader you can become."

24

Every person that crosses your path in life is equally as significant. If you value people based on what you can get in return, you will live a life lacking in fulfillment.

I was so proud of them all when we met for our next class together - not only had everyone made a point of meeting Sam, the invisible man in the hallway, they were sharing some of the things they learned about him in their short conversation with him.

That exercise demonstrated one of life's most valuable lessons – something I always keep in mind. Remember that, rather than view members of your audience as merely bodies taking up seats, you must learn to connect with them, genuinely care about them and learn a little about who they are as individuals.

When building your presentation, it is important to differentiate between your personal goals and your purpose in presenting to the audience. Once you truly care about your audience, you will be better able to make this distinction.

For example, some of your goals in presenting may be to market yourself, earn a living and practice your public speaking skills. Your purpose, on the other hand, could be to touch, inspire and motivate your audience; to plant a seed in everyone's mind and heart that will flourish in time to help them grow and realize their ideal lives.

While your goals and your purpose may not necessarily be that different, it is important to focus on your purpose, rather than what your personal goals happen to be at the moment you are communicating your message.

25

Two main reasons for focusing on your purpose over your goals during your presentation:

1. Your audience is intelligent and intuitive and can discern if you have a genuine interest in motivating them to be successful. They will connect to the content and delivery of your speech when they know you are sincere. If you are genuine and passionate about helping the audience it will come across in your presentation and the audience will be more receptive to your message.

2. Most importantly, your purpose and intent during your presentation is directly reflected in the strength and impact of your presentation. When you focus on truly caring for the growth of your audience, your presentation will have greater impact. This is the point where you will be able to tap into speaking from your heart.

Just like Sam, the invisible man in the hallway, the audience will be able to feel your sincerity and passion and, in turn, their minds and hearts will open to their potential.

> *"People do not care how much you know until they know how much you care."*

Understanding Your Audience
Due Diligence – Why Did His Presentation Fail?

I remember sitting in the audience listening to a speaker who had a beautiful presentation. He was a great presenter – full of passion, great stories and analogies and great presence on stage. The presentation, however, was a complete failure in the eyes of the audience. How could that be?

The speaker did not do due-diligence with regard to the audience he was addressing. He did not understand their specific needs and concerns, nor did he understand the critical messages the organizers were trying to relay. As great as the presentation was, it did not connect to the emotions, fears and concerns of the audience. As a result, the audience did not feel a connection. In short, they felt that they got a canned presentation.

Presenters need to link their message to the emotions that members of the audience experience day to day and connect each presentation to their specific experiences, fears, hopes and joys.

Due diligence can be done on endless topics - but when doing my due diligence, there is always one constant that I focus on, regardless of who the audience is or the topic I am presenting. That focus must be to understand the issues, pains, concerns, problems that members of the audience is facing on a daily basis.

27

Unless we can connect our message with our audience based on that, they will never feel that we truly understand what they are going through. *"Only when your audience feels heard and understood will they open their minds"* to listening to what you are trying to convey to them.

> *"Presenters need to link their message to the emotions*
> *that the members of the audience experience"*

Understanding your audience will help you customize your presentation so that it meets their needs. Gathering information regarding audience expectations is critical to preparing for your presentation.

- Who are the audience members?

- What is their mindset?

- What are their goals and motivations for attending the presentation?

Use the client who hired you as a resource for learning about your audience and their expectations. What does the client believe the audience is hoping to gain from the experience?

> **"The simplest way to customize is to phone members of the**
> **audience in advance and ask them what they expect from**
> **your session, and why they expect it.**
> **Then use their quotes throughout your presentation."**
> ***Alan Pease***

At the same time, if you have access to the audience members, take the opportunity to:

- Tap into their minds
- Find out what their expectations are
- Determine their needs
- Lean about their fears

Feeling understood is one of the human mind's greatest needs and understanding your target audience will help you shape a successful presentation.

Your audience needs to feel that you were speaking to each of them directly— something you can only achieve if you have done the appropriate research and learned their specific concerns and daily emotions.

Determining Objectives – What Happens in Vegas...

Las Vegas thrives on people who are willing to take a gamble. I know people that still talk about the win they had years ago. How they picked the right table, the right time and made the right decisions in order to create that win. It is amazing too, how others tend to speak about how one of their friends won a large gamble.

Then there are the stories that last within people's hearts forever – they impact everyone involved. They are the stories about the times when someone lost one of those gambles in Las Vegas - a large enough amount that you can feel your heart stop for what feels like a lifetime.

That feeling of fear, disappointment, betrayal, stupidity or humiliation is the exact feeling the organizer of any event or presentation is trying to avoid. It is their job to pick the right table and play the right game. As in Las Vegas where there are thousands of games to choose from – there are also a thousand possible speakers they can hire. It is an absolute gamble. They know that if they pick the wrong one it will impact everyone involved and, more importantly, it will be talked about for years to come – "Remember when John hired that speaker for our event, I can't believe it – what was he thinking hiring him..."

"Your audience needs to feel that you were speaking to each of them directly"

When you as the speaker determine the others objectives, all parties involved in the communication will win. The positive emotions experienced by your audience will be remembered and result in a ripple effect that will promote your name throughout the organization, their industry and the many speakers' outlets available to you.

This principle is the same whether you have been hired to deliver a keynote presentation to 1000 people or your boss has asked you to do a quick presentation to your co-workers.

Despite whatever feelings your client may have about the work involved in organizing the event, they will be motivated to ensure the session is successful - as the organizer, their name will be on the line. You are responsible for ensuring the person who asked you to speak has zero regrets - leave them eager to bring you back again.

Ask your client to tell you what they envision from the presentation. You can provide encouragement but, ultimately, you should make sure your client explicitly describes their expectations and the concept of what form the event should take.

This is important because it includes them in the process and forces them to take some ownership of the outcome. They will feel more comfortable with the process if they have some decision-making power, and they'll feel a sense of pride in the success of the event if they are involved in its organization. Only once you are aware of your client's objectives will you be in the position to impart your knowledge and guidance.

You might determine that the objectives your client initially expresses may not be what their true objectives should be. Never ask a client a question you would not be prepared to answer yourself for them. Be ready to suggest possible objectives for your client to consider - they may be at a loss or need you to guide them down the right path.

Last year I had an epiphany that I was going to start doing triathlons - even though I had not been on a bicycle in a decade, could not do much more than the dog paddle and had never run more than a 10km distance. I used to cycle a lot when I was younger so, with a little research on-line, I figured I knew everything I needed to in order to purchase a bicycle.

When I got to the bike shop, Mike, the sales person, started asking me questions that I was not sure how to respond. Once Mike saw that I was fumbling for answers, he offered suggestions that got me thinking along the right path again. I walked into that store believing I knew everything I needed to know – it was not until I heard the right questions that I learned what I really needed to know.

The same holds true when it comes to the organizers of events or our leaders asking us to do a presentation on something particular. Never assume what they say they want is the right thing for the audience. Learn to ask questions to confirm their thoughts and one of two things will happen.

1. You will have confirmed what they believed they wanted from you as a speaker.
2. They will realize that there were things they never thought about - things that may require more thought.

Either way, you will not only look like a professional but they will start relying on you as the expert.

Client Fears: 1 of 3 Reactions

When working with a client/organizer of an event, remember to keep their emotions in mind throughout the process.

"Their reputation is on the line as the moment they agree to hire you." Throughout the entire process, especially in the planning stages, you will have to keep the fears they will experience in mind.

You will need to tap into their experience regarding similar sessions, since that is where their positive and negative emotions arise when organizing future sessions.

Everyone who has engaged a speaker or facilitator for a presentation will have experienced one of three reactions:

1. Indifference – the speaker really made no impact.
2. Negativity – something the speaker did or said has made a long lasting negative impression.
3. Positive Optimism – something the speaker did or said that left them feeling the presentation was positive and successful.

What you can learn from your client about previous speakers will provide powerful insight. Find out what they liked, what they never want to experience again and what they would like to repeat. Once you know the answers to those questions, encourage your client to relive the emotions attached by bringing them back to that event that caused those emotions. Once your client knows that you understand the implications of those emotions they will tell you everything you need to know in order for you to build the most relevant and powerful presentation.

Working With Clients-
Death Of A Wedding DJ

When working with clients it is important to keep in mind that, in most cases, organizing the event is outside the scope of their daily job duties and, in some cases, they may view the work it takes to organize the event as an inconvenience.

Some clients will want you to keep them in the loop throughout the entire process; others may only require a summary at the end.

"Be sensitive to what works best for the individual."

To minimize the hassle, be prepared, flexible and sensitive to your client's preferences. Your client's time is valuable, so do not waste it. Bring a prepared set of questions for them; gathering as much information as possible up front will save time for you both.

34

Besides ensuring they are actively involved in the planning of the event, you should also encourage clients to express any concerns they may have so that you can address them and offer reassurances.

This will provide you with valuable information on what scenarios to avoid and give you a chance to reassure the client of your competence and make them feel comfortable.

No matter how much presentation experience you have compared to the client, you should always involve them in the planning process. It is crucial for making them feel comfortable and ensuring the outcome meets their expectations.

I recently attended the wedding of a close friend. The bride had arranged the best of the best for every element of her wedding so I was surprised when just a few days before the big day I heard her say "I am going to kill the DJ we hired." When I asked if the problem was that he was not as good as she expected she told me that he was the best for what she was looking for but he just would not keep her in the loop. I suggested that if she told me what was missing or what it was that she needed to know I would contact the DJ and have it taken care of.

"There is nothing wrong and I believe he will do a great job" she replied, "I just need him to keep in touch and reassure that he will be doing what I am expecting. I don't need you to bring me confirmation; I just need to hear it straight from him."

Her reply made perfect sense to me - the terms of her relationship with her DJ were consistent with the terms of a relationship between a speaker and an organizer.

Being involved gives your client ownership – they will feel more confident when they know what to expect. By keeping your client in the loop, you will eliminate the greatest fear an organizer has about hiring a speaker – the fear of the unknown.

Questions To Ask

To be or not to be: that is the question. At least, that is the question according to Shakespeare. This passage from Hamlet is often quoted, but not nearly considered enough. The beauty of Shakespeare's soliloquy in Hamlet is not so much about the answers it gives, but the questions it asks.

Effective questioning is an entire course, and an art in itself. *"Asking the right questions of your client will bring out the true concerns"*, issues and messages that need to cover in the session. Once you' have deciphered this critical information you can tailor a presentation, customizing it for the audience at hand.

Here are some examples of questions to ask your client:

1. Basic audience information

- How many people will attend?
- What are the roles of the attendees in the organization?
- What is the general age group?
- What is the gender breakdown?
- How much experience do they have in their positions?
- Where are they from (different cities/countries)?

2. Past client experience

- When was the last time you attended a course/seminar?
- Who was the presenter?
- What was the topic?
- What was the best part?
- What part, if any, would you change?

3. Desired situation

- What is the conference theme?
- What message do you want the audience to retain?
- What would make you say it was a successful session?
- Do you require a workbook/handouts/summaries etc.?
- Do you want more of a 'hands on' approach or a theoretical one?
- How and when do you want me to keep you in the loop as we build the session?
- What is the objective of the session/presentation?

Creating Content
Know Your Message- What's Your Point?

I n the movie Dumb and Dumber, Jim Carey's character Lloyd pines for Mary, played by Lauren Holly. Although it is clear that Lloyd is out of his league with Mary, he pursues her anyway. At one point, Mary tries to make her lack of interest very clear. When he asks her what his chances are with her, she tells him they're about one in a million.

This rejection is clear and to the point, but Lloyd says, "So you're tellin' me there's a chance."

This classic line is one of the most famous from the movie, because we can all laugh at how completely and thoroughly Lloyd has missed the point of what Mary is trying to say.

While Lloyd is a silly character in a raucous comedy, his ability to listen to someone trying to tell him one thing and walk away hearing something different is not a problem limited to fiction. People misinterpret things every day, from simple conversations to large media stories. While some of this failure certainly rests with the person digesting the information, there is also often room for improvement from the source.

In presentations, therefore, *"you need to make sure that you are clear and certain in your message"* in order to ensure that the audience walks away with the intended impression.

Establish one to three main points you want to convey to the audience and ensure they are Principle-Based. Any principle-based message will be relevant to all aspects of their lives, including both business and personal situations.

"Create stories and analogies to get the message across in an entertaining and meaningful way."

Do not merely put words to your message or your audience will leave feeling that they might as well just read it in a book. The best way to keep your audience emotionally engaged and interested in what you have to say is to provide real-life examples and some entertainment value.

We have all heard the saying that people may not remember what you told them, but they will always remember how you made them feel.

As a presenter, if you can make your audience feel an emotion associated with your message, they will remember it forever. That is what the term Principle-Based refers to – connecting your audience to a principle is relevant in any communication and any area in their life.

Learn The Client's Message

Determine with your client one to three main points they would like the audience to grasp. Ensure the messages are universal and principle-based so they can apply to any, and all, aspects of their lives.

Link Your Message To Theirs
– You Are The Sole Survivor In Your City

You have a message/story/philosophy you would like to share. Similarly, your client has hired you to communicate a message they want to share.

Select stories and analogies that are consistent with your client's message and your own philosophy, and shape these in a way that demonstrates to your audience how they relate to their personal and professional lives.

I was speaking to a group of people working in the medical profession focusing on heart attack patients and prevention. One of the messages I wanted to share was about the number of people that die of heart attacks every year so, instead of just verbalizing that statistic, I told a story - an analogy about the very city where the presentation was taking place. Coincidently, the population of that city was close to the number of people who die of heart attacks every year.

This is how I shared my message: "Imagine waking up tomorrow morning to discover that you are the sole survivor in the city where you live. Would you think you have an epidemic on your hands?"

"Starting the message with
an impactful analogy gets their attention."

When you are preparing the content of your presentation, keep in mind that if you got to your message immediately, spouting statistics and spelling details out

40

for your audience without any anecdotes or metaphors, the presentation would be no more relevant than if they were to read a book. There is little likelihood that your message will have meaning or relevance to them - they would retain very little.

It is through stories and anecdotes that you can really reach listeners and give them something to think about. When you are writing your stories and anecdotes, keep them relevant to each message and structure them so that they build up to the message you want to convey

Research The Topic

Once you have learned the message your client would like delivered, and have thought about how to combine it with your own approach and message on the subject, you should do some additional research on the topic so that you are up to speed.

You do not want the audience to catch you by surprise. Increase your knowledge about the topic you are presenting by reading up on it as much as possible. Research the internet, visit the library and, most importantly, discuss it with as many people as possible.

By discussing your topic, you will encounter some of the different objectives and viewpoints that the audience could potentially throw your way during your presentation. This process will help you refine your message.

Make use of whatever information you can get your hands on. Even if you do not end up using it specifically in your presentation, it may come in handy for the Q&A sessions with the audience.

Organize Your Content

Organize your content according to the message you are sharing with the audience. Your message should include only a few specific main points.

Using Quotations, Facts, Statistics

Telling someone that working out is good for them is true. However, for most people, hearing that truth isn't usually enough to make a difference in their life. On the other hand, if you tell someone that working out can lower your risk of cardiovascular disease by 50 percent and can reduce your risk of premature death by 40 percent, then they are far more likely to make a lifestyle change.

Any quotations, facts and statistics used should be current and relevant to the audience, market, industry and demographics. Always link them to a story, situation or example to emphasize the point you are making. Do not bombard your audience with charts or graphs; use quotations, facts and statistics sparingly and select only the ones that highlight your message

"Any quotations, facts and statistics used should be current and relevant to the audience"

Bring some life to statistics by connecting them to something that your audience can be visualize or experience through emotion, as in the example about the number of deaths due to heart attacks, so that your audience feels the impact at an emotional level.

"Bring some life to statistics by connecting them to something that your audience can be visualize or experience through emotion"

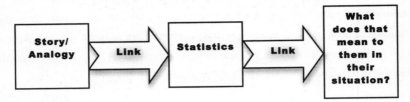

As a speaker, you must be very clear in your mind and heart when it comes to your principled messages.

Link the messages to your client's messages through:

- **Stories**

- **Analogies**

- **Statistics**

- **Quotes**

Always be fully aware of the impact each of these will have on your audience.

"He uses statistics as a drunken man uses lamp-posts...
for support rather than illumination."

Andrew Lang (1844-1912)

Appropriate Technology

"Technology can be your best friend, or your worst enemy."
Fred Sarkari

Many years ago when I was first starting out and was still developing the process of creating my presentations, I stumbled upon a new software program that was supposed to be top of the line. It promised to make the time I spent creating my presentations so much more productive, easier and less time consuming and I was so excited to get my hands on a product that was going to help me create phenomenal presentations. It truly was the best software at its time; the output of visual presentations it could create was like watching a CSI agent delivering a presentation to his colleagues.

Now came the time to use the technology. As it turned out, there were parts of the software that I was very comfortable using and I found it to be quite effective. Then there was the rest of it; after hours, weeks and months, I realized I was trying to use technology that I was not comfortable with and, in the end, it did nothing but waste more of my time.

My point here is that when you use the right technology for you it can do wonders for your business, but when you use technology that might be right for your business but not you as a person than it can be a disaster – wasting time, energy and causing frustration.

45

Visual Aids

"Visual aids heighten retention of information - by up to 70%."

Using visual aids through technology is like taking vitamins for your body - enhancing performance while maintaining the essential needs.

Technology and visual aids should never replace the dynamic power of you, the presenter; they should serve to heighten your presentation skills.

"Memorable presenters will engage as many of the audience's senses as possible, and encourage audience participation."

Tony Buzan

Following are Tony Buzan's figures on the subject of retention of information as it pertains to how we receive information:

- **Read 10%**
- **Heard 20%**
- **Seen 30%**
- **Heard and Seen 50%**
- **Said 70%**
- **Said and Done 90%**

Following are aids you would use in most presentations and a few essentials you should keep in mind.

PowerPoint-
Read Me A Bedtime Story

As far as design is concerned, focus on what is audience appropriate. Keep it simple but do not be simplistic.

"People are visual so slides should relay the message you are trying to get across"

People are visual so slides should relay the message you are trying to get across, for example with a picture or a simple graph. Refrain from visual aids that are particularly flashy as they may be distracting and could potentially divert attention from what you are saying.

"Do not use PowerPoint as a teleprompter to read your speech."

The audience is not there to have a bedtime story read to them nor are they there to read a book pasted on your PowerPoint presentation. Keep visual content to a minimum. Remember, the slides are there merely to complement your stories and messages. Whenever possible, try to use pictures to complement your presentation. When you need to use content, do not exceed 6 to 7 lines of text. Short sentences and bullet points work best.

*"For the sake of the audience's sanity,
avoid using every function available in PowerPoint."*

47

PowerPoint Tips:

- Keep it simple but do not be simplistic
- Refrain from flashy visual aids
- Keep slides simple, clear and short
- Use bullet points instead of sentences
- PowerPoint is not a Teleprompter
- Keep content to a minimum
- Use pictures
- Do not exceed 6 to 7 lines of text
- Do not over use transitions

"My 9 year old nephew made a PowerPoint,
he used clipart, and it was cute."

Fred Sarkari

Flip charts and Eraser Boards:

Flip charts are a great way to get people off their seats and moving. Remember, movement creates energy and energy ignites thought.

I prefer flip charts to eraser boards as you can give the audience the content on the flip chart at the end of the presentation. Flipcharts can also be taped anywhere in the room or, more importantly, they can be taken to different breakout sessions.

Microphones – Oops!
Can Anyone Hear Me?

Lapel microphones are great for those presenters who are very energetic and rely on a lot of movement on stage.

You will want to keep your hands free whenever possible during your presentation and will find that a lapel microphone is preferable to a hand held microphone.

Make sure there is someone there that knows how to control the volume just in case you need it changed in the middle of the presentation. You do not want to be the one going back and forth playing with the technology.

I remember listening to one particular presenter - she was amazing. She had the crowd engaged and energized. I was taking pages of notes, not only on her content but also what made her such a great presenter.

As she spoke, she continued to build momentum – her audience engaged and energized. Suddenly her mic began cutting out, stalling the momentum she had built. It was her responsibility to control the mic and she had no choice but to stop her presentation, fix the problem and then attempt to build momentum all over again.

I recently faced a similar situation where my mic cut out – fortunately, I had arranged for someone to handle the technical aspects of my presentation and was back on track within seconds.

"A great presentation is the result of
The momentum built throughout –
Stopping the momentum
Stops the energy within the presentation."

Notes

Action Plan:

List 3 Critical Messages
you want to take away from this Chapter.

1.

2.

3.

Preparation

*"It takes one hour of preparation
for each minute of presentation time."*
Wayne Burgraff

The Boxing Ring Never Lies

C onfidence is nothing more than trusting in yourself and feeling good about what you are doing. Having confidence does not mean you will not be nervous - it means even though you are nervous you will do it anyway. It is okay to be nervous, it will drive you.

There are a few key ways to build confidence when it comes to doing presentations.

> *"Knowing, rather than memorizing, your topic will strengthen your confidence."*

Increase your knowledge about the topic you are presenting by researching it as much as you can. Practice speaking about your topic, discuss it with other people, - you might even try taking different sides and explore a different point of view.

Go through different scenarios and discussions to prepare for anything an audience member may throw your way.

1. **Know your topic rather than memorizing your speech**
2. **Continuously research your topic**
3. **Discuss your topic with others**
4. **Take different viewpoints of your topic during discussions**
5. **Most importantly, just go ahead and speak**

Speak with more confidence than you may actually feel. If your audience believes you are confident they will be less likely to challenge you, in fact they will listen to you intently.

In order to build confidence at the beginning of a presentation, talk to your audience, have a casual discussion, tell a story... interacting in this way will help you to relax.

Confidence ultimately comes with real-life practice - after all, there are only so many hours you can spend rehearsing in front of the mirror; the best practice takes place on stage.

"A great presentation is the result of the momentum built throughout"

55

Sandy, a good friend of mine, and a former professional fighter, once shared an important philosophy with me. "The boxing ring never lies."

What he was saying is that you can practice all you want on a punching bag and in front of a mirror but until you actually step into the ring, you will never know what skill level you are at – you will never know who you are as a fighter.

That message is so very relevant to presenters. We can practice all we want in front of a mirror and our pets, but until we are willing to step out on that stage, we will never know who we are as presenters.

Fear –
An Olympian Will Crash If...

"Great presenters are not slaves of their fear,
They are masters of their fear".

When we are afraid, we put up walls to protect ourselves. This is instinctual but it does not mean we cannot learn to adapt and deal with our fears in other ways. The protective walls erected by fear inhibit us from being our authentic selves. While stress and fear will undoubtedly plague every speaker from time to time, it is important to remember that it is in those moments that we must be most conscious of being our true self.

"The greatest detriment to any speaker is doubt."

A negative thought is more powerful and can cause more damage than a positive thought. You can overcome doubt by visualizing a flawless delivery and train your mind to eliminate any sense of uncertainty from your heart and mind.

A creative acronym for FEAR is:

False
Evidence
Appearing
Real

You are not alone if the thought of speaking in public scares you. Giving a presentation to an audience regularly tops the list in surveys of top fears. Even experienced speakers feel their heart thumping when they step on stage.

In the beginning, you may fear:

- **Your topic**

- **Your presentation**

- **Your audience**

Initially these three items are unknown and you will not have had enough experience with these variables to feel comfortable. As you become more familiar with your presentation and topic, your fear in relation to them will lessen. A bit of fear however, will always remain when it comes to the audience, as it will always be an unknown to you.

We all have fear of standing in front of people. The term 'fear of public speaking' is in fact one of the biggest fallacies. People are not afraid of public speaking, people are simply experiencing one of the greatest fears of the human mind that is *linked* to public speaking – the fear of the unknown, the greatest fear of the human mind.

For an experienced speaker, their presentation, style, message etc. are no longer the unknowns.

What you will not know is your audience their state of mind, what kind of a day they have had...

This is where, as experienced speakers, *"we have to believe in our message and we have to be authentic."* The principle is the same for both experienced and novice speakers.

The fear felt by speakers and presenters results from the unknown. Even experienced speakers have no idea how a particular audience will react and respond to them as a presenter. The most important strategy to overcome fear is to start presenting. Do not allow fear to hold you back. Do not wait until you think you will be perfectly ready because that time will never come. With every presentation you deliver, you will grow and refine your style.

"The fear of the unknown, the greatest fear of the human mind"

If you are apprehensive about delivering a presentation, change your state of mind - Visualize a perfect presentation and you will turn any sense of fear to excitement.

If an Olympian bobsledder focuses on crashing or missing a turn, he will crash. If he visualizes every corner and straight section of the track and makes a mental plan - he knows exactly how the race will go. A downhill skier plans their exact path down the hill, every edge carved into the snow before pushing off. Similarly, as a great presenter you will need to visualize the emotions your audience will experience and 'see' their positive responses to your message.

"Change how you look at people
and the people you look at will change."

59

I practiced my first presentation for months, I knew the presentation inside out and backwards, yet I found every excuse to convince myself I was not ready. Then the day came when I had to step up to the plate.

The presentation should have lasted anywhere from 45 min to 1.5 hours depending on the interaction of the audience.
I was so prepared that I knew I was going to blow the mind of everyone in the room - I was going to make an impact they would talk about for years.

When I got up to speak, I opened with a great introduction... for my first presentation. Then I immediately lost all recollection of the content of my entire presentation - except for the conclusion. So that is what I did, I concluded.

I lasted for 7 minutes in front of what at the time seemed like a large audience of 10 people! It was fortunate for me that someone got up, covered for me by saying that I was only giving them an overview and finished off the presentation.

"Visualize a perfect presentation and you will turn any sense of fear to excitement"

In the end, no matter how much you practice in front of the mirror, you have to be willing to just step up to the plate. My greatest fear hit me flat in the face – that night I had a decision to make – get out and speak again tomorrow or let the fear over-take my DNA and most likely never speak again. My fear was greater than most of you will experience but I knew that if I did not get on stage to do something within the twenty-four hours, I probably never would again. The next day I introduced another speaker to a group of 15 people and I rebuilt from there. In turn, my destiny evolved from my greatest fear.

Always plant the seed of positive thought in your mind prior to each presentation. Do not discourage yourself by thinking of all the things that might go wrong.

"The best way to prepare your mind for success is to visualize your perfect presentation."

Visualize your style, your movement, your speech and the response of your audience. If you are positive about your presentation it will help you work toward making it better and the more you work at it the better you will become.

"You have to be willing to just step up to the plate"

Visualize:

- Your Style

- Your Movement

- Ideal response from your audience

- Your speech

- Your Body Language

- Smiles in the audience

- Laughter and enjoyment in the audience

Effective preparation is the key to achieving confidence, which, in turn, is a key element to your success. Effective preparation consists of many components and is more than just good content.

Effective preparation and rehearsal will reduce your nervousness by 75% and increase the likelihood of avoiding errors to 95%. (Source: the Fred Pryor Organization - a significant provider of seminars and open presentation events)

Fear is an emotion generated by your thoughts at a particular moment in time. Change your language in your mind and you will change your state of mind, and in turn, you will change the emotions that you are feeling.

"Visualizing success will bring you a step closer to achieving success."

You likely have heard many elaborate tips for overcoming the fear of public speaking. The best tip I can give you is very simple: practice, practice and practice some more. When I say practice, I am not saying look in the mirror and hit the punching bag. Step over those ropes and step on the stage.

Then, when you think you have practiced enough, practice again. Your presentation skills will be continually evolving; practice is what facilitates that evolution.

"The best way to improve your public speaking skills is to face your fears head on"

Timing Your Speech –
Ideas Flow When Speaking To Your Cat

Remember that you will inevitably speak faster on stage than during your practice runs. That might change as you gain more experience.

You might practice at home and find that your ideas flow for a full ten minutes, but on stage that flow might last only three minutes. That is because at home, you are usually speaking to yourself or to a non-threatening audience – your cat for example. When we speak without inhibition or fear our thoughts flow best.

Two things can happen on stage; you can speak too fast and not connect your message to your audience or, you can go to the other end of the spectrum and babble on without ever getting to the message.

The best way to practice is to tape your practice sessions. In doing so, you can imagine yourself on stage as you listen to your own voice. You will hear where you need to lengthen your story or, at times, shorten it.

To overcome the timing challenge, break things down. If you have twenty slides with three main messages, time each message separately. It is always better to have more than less; you might not use it all but your audience will be none the wiser!

Time various scenarios. For example, if I have a very interactive audience compared to one that is not as responsive I will still be able to fill the time with my material.

The most crucial thing is to never exceed your allotted time. If you are to finish at 5 pm then you should be completely done and people should be able to walk out at 5 pm. If people expect to finish at a certain time they will make plans and have appointments.

More importantly, your audience will start shutting down their minds to you toward the end of the presentation, they start thinking about what lies ahead, the reality of what they have to get back to; be it work related or personal. If you run on too long, you run the risk that your audience will miss out on your concluding message,

If you hold them longer than the committed time, they are also likely to get antsy, stop listening and even feel resentful. Respect other people's time and honor your commitment to be done by the allotted time, and you will retain your credibility.

"Never exceed your allotted time"

How to Practice –
Muhammad Ali Style

"Great presenters are created; this creation evolves through consistent practice.

The more presentations you give, the more you will develop your own personal presentation style."

Fred Sarkari

I must say that I sometimes get tired of hearing the word visualize - visualize your way to success, visualize the perfect presentation and now you have created your path to success... Wow, if only it really was that easy!

Visualization is merely the most basic first step.

In order for visualization to work, you must understand the science behind it. The greatest athletes in the world win their gold in their heads before the start of the race. A big part of their training is comprised of mental preparation.

Muhammad Ali, the greatest boxer of all time, was famous for playing mind games with himself. He had such control over his thoughts that, before ever stepping into the ring, every molecule in his body had already won the fight.

Of course, he did the obvious things that most of us do; words of affirmation, telling ourselves we are the best, we will rock the crowd,

66

visualize your audience having a great time. Ali went beyond that - he visualized every second of that fight, every movement, each blink of the eye and shift of the head.

Speakers often make a big mistake by thinking they just need to visualize a successful presentation. Some will go as far as seeing the audience clapping, laughing and enjoying themselves. They then enter the danger zone where they visualize the positive minor responses and reactions of the audience when, in fact, that does nothing but hinder their performance.

When visualizing the audience you should only go as far as an Olympic Gold medalist visualizing the crowd in order to get excited during training. When they step out on the competitive field, all their focus is on themselves.

"before ever stepping into the ring, every molecule in his body had already won the fight"

Instead of typical audience visualization, as a presenter you need to think of yourself as an athlete and focus on self-visualization. Visualizing your audience without first focusing on yourself will do nothing but hinder your performance since you will be reacting to anything and everything your audience does. All athletes know that, to play your best game, you must direct all your focus on your performance.

"Practice needs to simulate the actual event in your mind's eye."

This is where the practice comes into play – You will need to rehearse not merely the words, but the feelings we want the audience to experience. You will also need to get a sense of what you will be feeling while you are on stage.

"As speakers, we ourselves need to be able to feel every emotion we want our audience to feel."

We need to know first-hand, in every molecule of our body, the feelings of pain, hurt, love, happiness, anger etc. before we can expect our audience to do so.

Your brain does not know the difference between thinking about doing something and actually doing it. Remember this very critical fact!

It does not know the difference between practice and the actual event. This is why it is imperative that your rehearsals duplicate your actual events precisely as you intend to have them occur on stage. You will need to know every word and every feeling behind those words.

You can practice your speech, your style, body language, tone of voice... but you cannot practice authenticity – you just are. When you practice, visualize and live the actual event in your mind.

"Visualizing your audience without first focusing on yourself will do nothing but hinder your performance"

Imagine giving a speech to your dog or cat. You are not concerned in the least about hecklers or criticism and you can fully trust that they will not find fault or judge what you believe or whom you are – you are free to share openly and passionately. This is being authentic, and authenticity is what will connect you to your audience.

**"It is quite simple really –
to be your best, you just need to be yourself."**

Novice speakers who try to imitate a speaker who has impressed them in the past are usually disappointed and left trying to figure out what went wrong. Instead of trying to be the next Anthony Robbins, stop faking it and build on your own strengths, connect to who you are, and let that authenticity lead you to become the best speaker you can be.

"Your brain does not know the difference between thinking about doing something and actually doing it"

Great presenters with great messages who do not come across as being authentic are perceived by their audience as calculating or insincere - regardless of the fact that they may have rehearsed to the point of perfection and planned on duplicating what they achieved in the living room when they step on stage. Like the best-laid plans of mice and men, the best-rehearsed speeches often go awry. Once an audience's perception is established, no amount of preparation can counter it.

69

"When you are authentic with your intentions, the individuals in the audience mirror that authenticity."

Minds, hearts, stories and journeys become one, creating the opportunity for them to live your presentation.

Remember that when you practice, do so with as much passion as possible. Select a message and work on it until you have refined it so it is not too long yet still makes the point; then keep repeating it until it flows naturally and without hesitation, like reciting the alphabet.

"Let that authenticity lead you to become the best speaker you can be."

Alphabet Principle of Practice:

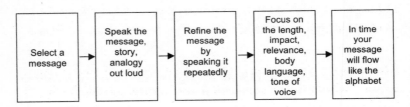

Remember key words for your stories and messages. Those key words should link you to the entire message in your mind. Have your PowerPoint slides printed out and practice frequently with them in front of you. When you are on stage and you see the slide on the screen you want that recognition to occur immediately, you want your memory triggered without a moment's hesitation.

70

Tap into your voice. Try speaking with energy when you are at home, using different parts of your voice and, in time, you will know which one works for you.

"When you practice, do so with as much passion as possible"

Go to a place where no one can hear you, pick a story you want to share, turn on a tape recorder and pretend you are presenting.

As you play it back, listen to one section at a time and ask yourself if there is life behind your words, is your tone of voice appropriate etc. Try it again with more life and energy. Repeat this process until you feel there is life behind your story and you are certain your audience will feel and live your analogy.

Great athletes always have a coach. Great presenters should always have a coach as well. In order to be your best you have to work with the best. One thing every professional has in common is that they work with a coach – they know a coach will see things they never will.

Once you have developed a reasonable amount of comfort with your presentation, ask a friend or a family member to listen to it and provide constructive feedback.

The amount of time and work you will have to put in to make your presentation a success may seem overwhelming but, if the success of one presentation is not sufficient to validate the work, consider this: when you learn to speak well, you will sell your ideas and, in turn, be a better communicator and a better leader. Developing excellent communication skills is one of the cornerstones of becoming successful in many aspects of life at work and even at home.

Making Cheat Notes

"I use many props.
The props act as cue cards reminding me
of what to say next."

Tom Ogden

When an athlete takes to the field, it is his time to put all of his hard work and practice into performance. With everything on the line, there are no second chances and the stakes are always high. However, even the best athletes don't go into situations blind. They have fallback cues to help them stay on track. Base coaches provide insight for runners. Football linemen look for movement on the line of scrimmage to figure out which areas to cover. Basketball players call different plays to set up their offense more effectively.

These small cues serve as prompts to help keep athletes focused and on the path for success. Public speakers can incorporate similar cues, or cheat notes, into their presentation, in order to build confidence and keep the presentation on track.

72

"Great athletes always have a coach. Great presenters should always have a coach"

There are a few ways to make cheat notes:

1. Slides

Use pictures on your slides that represent the story or message you want to share. Pictures are a lot easier to remember; they alleviate the need to memorize a story.

2. Cue-cards

Your cue cards should only have one or two words, in large font that will trigger your memory for what you want to say. Never write out sentences unless you plan to read your speech.

3. Printed slides

"Write down one word that will trigger what you want to say" below each slide. If possible, have a table beside you where you can lay out your cheat notes. Write the words in large letters so you can see the word from a distance, at a glance.

Check It Twice And Pack It Up

In carpentry, expert builders know to measure twice and cut once. When working with wood, making a mistake wastes time and materials, which can ultimately jeopardize the integrity of the entire product.

Presentations are much the same way. Leaving materials behind or bringing items that malfunction can significantly impede your focus and negatively affect your overall performance.

Have a checklist of everything that you need for the presentation.

Take a complete inventory, check it twice and, most importantly, pack it up the night before.

Checklists are the key to preparing in advance and avoiding glitches and delays - we use them for all major events, from the expected birth of a child to preparing for a vacation. When we are excited or anxious, the likelihood that something might be forgotten goes up significantly.

You will have other things to concentrate on the day of the presentation. Prepare a list of the things that you will need both before and during your presentation in finite detail so you are free to focus and stay in the moment when you are delivering your presentation.

74

Dress Code –
Sexy Lingerie

"They expect a professional presentation,
so they expect to see a professional.
Dress appropriately for the occasion,
but don't be one of the crowd."

Wess Roberts

People like to say that it's what's on the inside that counts. While there is some truth to this, if people can't get over your outward appearance, they will never pay attention long enough to find out what is on the inside. What you wear is representative of who you are, and you should dress in a way that reflects confidence and comfort.

There are a few ways to look at a dress code. If you feel comfortable, you will look comfortable no matter what you wear. I have met presenters who show more confidence and command the stage in shorts and T-shirts than those wearing a custom fit $2000 suit.

If you are able to captivate your audience, then it does not matter what you wear. That said, it is a good idea to avoid wearing clothes that are very bright and flashy, unless they are part of your style and presentation, as they can be visually distracting for the audience. Wear calm colors and not too many different colors or flashy accessories. People get distracted very easily. You want them to focus on your presentation, not your clothes.

75

Overall, it is a good idea to mirror the audience to which you are speaking.

Anything you can do as far as your appearance goes will boost your confidence. For women, there are studies that have proven that, regardless of how she chooses to dress on the outside, wearing new, sexy lingerie boosts her confidence by 40%

Most critical aspect of your dress code is to make sure you feel comfortable and confident in what you wear.

"If you feel comfortable, you will look comfortable no matter what you wear"

Notes

Action Plan

Write 3 Critical Messages
you want to take away from this Chapter.

1. _____

_____

2. _____

_____

3. _____

_____

Presenting

*"Ask a heckler to identify himself and his company.
They usually prefer to be anonymous."*
Judy Moreo

What I learned from a Monk

Rene Descartes was a 17th century philosopher who changed the course of modern thought with one simple sentence: "I think, therefore I am." Known widely in Latin as cogito ergo sum, this concept puts a focus on the power of thought to define ourselves and the world around us. Though years have passed, we would all do well to remember Descartes' theory, especially when it comes to giving a presentation.

Your thoughts will undoubtedly affect your reality and, more importantly, they will affect the reality of those in your audience. The best tool you can have as a speaker is power over your thoughts, before, during and after your presentation.

"When you implant authentic thoughts, your entire reality and the reality of your audience will transform."

Every thought you have is a physical energy that reveals itself through your physical self on stage therefore, your thoughts are more effective than words when it comes to influencing others. One interpretation of the power of thought is a flow of energy between objects. Just as energy exists in nature, connecting each molecule to another, your thoughts, when pure and authentic, will connect you to each audience member. When you achieve this, you will have attained the power of a collective

80

and will have the power of your intention on stage multiplied and flowing throughout the entire room and every individual in it.

Everyone has heard the adage people may not remember what you say, but they will never forget how you make them feel. Science shows that a focused thought has the ability to change the molecular structure of an object. Imagine how your thoughts can affect the thoughts of others in the room. You can alter their state of mind and change how they feel.

In everything we do, even before entering the room, our thoughts and intentions precede us. We have already started to influence others' state of mind before ever uttering a word. Although every movement we make might not necessarily make sense or fully comprehended by everyone else, they will undoubtedly feel it.

What I Learned From a Monk
Made Me a Better Presenter

I remember studying with a monk for a few months. He had the ability to heat water with his thoughts. When I asked how he did that, his simple answer was "this is truly the power of authentic thought - I focused on how I want that water to feel."

"People may not remember what you say, but they will never forget how you make them feel"

Your thoughts are and will always be your greatest tool on stage. It is imperative that we maintain full awareness and consciousness of the feelings we want to project while on stage. Since your intention has such an effect on your audience, you cannot fake this. You have to be authentic with your intentions to make a difference in the minds and hearts of your audience.

Bio –
Who Are You?

When someone has bad news to share, they might preface it by reminding the audience to not shoot the messenger. Have you ever thought about what that saying means? Just think about when you hear bad news. It doesn't matter where it comes from, your immediate response is to lash out at the person giving you the information, whether or not they are responsible. The saying actually derived from ancient times, when news often had to be relayed by a human envoy. Because of the risk these individuals faced on a daily basis, many towns and countries made it treason to harm the town crier.

Fortunately, when giving a presentation, you are not likely to face death, even if people don't like what you have to say. However, any time you stand in front of a group of people, it really is a little bit about you. No matter what your message is, the audience needs to engage with you as a presenter and as a person. While prepping the heart of your content is critical for overall success, it is important to remember that the messenger matters, too.

At some point, you will likely need to provide your bio, so it is best to have a few prepared in advance. Your audience needs to know who you are, what have you done and why are you standing there? Create a several bios, each one intended for a different purpose. Having them ready beforehand will save you the trouble of scrambling to produce one in a hurry when you need it.

Recommended types of bios:

- Main Bio
- Media Friendly Bio
- Introduction by a client
- Self-Introduction

Main Bio

Your main bio should be no longer than one page and should include the details of your accomplishments as well as what you have to offer clients. You are your product, so the aim of the bio should be to create confidence in your credibility and experience.

Media-Friendly Bio

Create a bio for media that clients can download; it should be a snapshot of what you do. The structure should consist of short, concise sentences and should include your contact information. Your media-bio should be just enough to capture the viewer's interest with a quick browse.

Your media bio should address the following:

- Any tangible results you have created for yourself and others
- Your main topic/area of expertise
- Companies you have worked with
- You presentation style
- What makes you different
- What are the benefits of working with you

Bio For Introduction By A Client

Prepare a bio for use by those who will be introducing you; it should be short and describe your relevant accomplishments. It should speak to your credibility and give substance to why the audience should listen to you.

List some of the clients with whom you have worked. You should also mention facts about your presentation style, for example if you have an interactive style or if you require the audience to take notes.

It is a good idea to use larger font with extra spacing between lines so the person introducing you can easily read the information.

Bio For Self-Introduction

Ideally, it is better to have your client introduce you, but it is a good idea to prepare a bio for introducing yourself in case it is required.

State your qualifications, but do so modestly. Focus less on promoting yourself and more on setting the stage for your presentation and the tone for the session.

Prepare the audience members for your expectations of them during the session, be sure to let them know what you would like them to consider and the behavioral guidelines they are to follow. For example, save questions to the end, ask questions at anytime, challenge my ideas, keep an open mind, laugh, have fun etc.

Beginning Your Speech- Audience Is Not Sympathetic To...

"It was the best of times, it was the worst of times."

Most people can identify the source of this line without even being literary scholars. This opening line from Charles Dickens' classic "A Tale of Two Cities" is so iconic that it has become part of a worldwide lexicon.

This is the power of a strong beginning. As a presenter, it is important to know that the first word you utter will set the tone for the rest of the presentation - for better or for worse.

As the time to start your presentation nears, it is important to pay attention to your state of mind. This is the point in time where most presenters focus on what could go wrong. What you need to concentrate on is visualizing your perfect presentation: how you will sound; how you will look; how the audience will respond; and the impact you will make in their hearts and minds.

A lot of books and courses state that the audience is sympathetic and wants to hear what you have to say. A few are, but most in the audience are not - they are there because either it is mandatory to attend or they are hoping that this speaker will be different from the rest.

Most people in your audience have sat through so many sessions that they have lost their sympathy and empathy and are more concerned with their return on time invested. Their mentality is that if you are willing to step up on stage you are an expert, not only on your topic, but as a presenter and communicator as well. Audience expectations have risen to new heights and it is up to you not to just meet but exceed those expectations.

Either way, most enter the room with a negative state of mind. Thoughts such as:

- What will he or she teach me that I do not already know?
- Not another presentation!
- What makes the speaker an expert in my field?

They will be remembering being disappointed with past presentations. It is imperative to ensure that you connect with their emotions in a different way. You can accomplish this by using appropriate jargon, technical terms, emotions, life experiences, their experiences and, most importantly, knowing when to use each of the above.

"A child-like passion will transform a presentation from informational to inspirational."

Presentation Formula
Block Buster Movie

Avoid the Typical Presentation Model

Back when I was working in the corporate sector, like most of you, I attended many presentations. One particular conference for the financial industry always comes to mind when I think of energy in a presentation. Before even arriving we had already been talking about how boring the topic and speakers would be.

The first speaker, a lawyer, started with his presentation with an introduction that sounded as if he was asking us to prepare for a long, boring hour. Throughout the presentation he stuck to his commitment to be boring and during his conclusion, he reminded us of how boring he was by summarizing it to us.

The topic had nothing to do with the poor impact of the presentation - I have heard the same topic in the past by presenters who made it engaging, fun and memorable; it was the delivery and model that killed it.

Once the presenter understands the *Presentation Formula,* which I will review with you soon, any topic can leave a lasting impression.

When it comes to the majority of presenters, the introduction, body and conclusion of the presentation provide a triple opportunity to bore the audience completely.

Typical Presentation Formula...

Introduction: Your introduction tells them you are going to bore them.

Body of the presentation: You actually bore them based on your promise to do so in the introduction.

Conclusion: In the end, you remind them by telling them how you bored them.

"Most of the presentations I have seen
I would rather have watched two men fish.
And I don't even fish."

Ideal Presentation Formula

A dynamic presentation taps into the minds of your audience but, more importantly, touches their heart, creates fun and leaves a lasting impression. The following presentation model will help you achieve that.

Introduction: Movie Trailer

- Entice their minds
- Create curiosity and excitement

Body: Emotional Roller Coaster

- Play the movie
- Exceed the expectations of the trailer by connecting to their emotions
- Engage all spectrums of their emotions

Conclusion: Crystallizing the Close

- Summarize the content in relation to the audience's situation
- Crystallize the main messages into their hearts

"A dynamic presentation not only taps into the minds of your audience but, more importantly, touches their heart"

Introduction
Movie Trailer

The introduction of a presentation is like a trailer of a new blockbuster movie. It excites the audience to want to see the movie, the presentation.

When the trailer comes out it catches your attention, stopping your mind from whatever it was thinking, drawing all your attention to what is on the screen. The trailer or introduction for your presentation needs to engage the minds and curiosity of your audience, exciting them with a greater value than any other thoughts in their minds at that moment in time.

When preparing your introduction, remember to appeal to your audience both mentally and emotionally. Create curiosity and excitement about what they are about to hear so that they are eager to sit and listen.

As with an exciting trailer for a movie, your goal is to give your audience a jolt that will get their attention and clear their minds of whatever stray thoughts they were entertaining before you began to speak. A good introduction will capture the audience's attention and imagination, setting the tone for what is to come. If you capture your listeners' attention with your introduction, you will have a better chance of keeping them on board as your presentation continues.

Body of the Presentation
Emotional Roller Coaster

Whereas your introduction is comparable to the trailer to a movie, the body of the presentation constitutes the movie itself. The body of the presentation should exceed the expectations set by the introduction.

The best blockbuster movies engage audience emotions at all times, taking them on an emotional rollercoaster or sensory adventure where they laugh, feel love, pain and live within the movie itself, often envisioning themselves as the lead character!

The same holds true for a blockbuster presenter – you need to take your audience on a roller coaster ride of emotions- love, pain, laughter, hurt, empathy and vision, allowing them to live within your presentation. Then and only then will they have a lifetime connection with your presentation – you will have left a lasting impression not only in their minds but in their hearts as well.

"A good introduction will capture the audience's attention and imagination"

To do this effectively, your content must reach the emotions of the audience members, such that they can visualize and identify with what you have to say.

The key to the presentation is to engage as many emotions within your audience as possible.

"Remember to appeal to your audience both mentally and emotionally"

Conclusion
Crystallize the Close

Your conclusion is your final chance to make an impression - whatever you deliver at the end will be freshest in the minds of your audience as they leave and will have a bearing on their overall assessment of the presentation.

The conclusion of a blockbuster movie touches the audience within their own lives. They feel the conclusion of the movie, be it love, pain, hurt, conquest or loss - the same results you should achieve with the summary of your presentation. Your summary needs to make a connection to your audience – something that relates to their life situations, not merely a summary of the words you spoke.

"Your content must reach the emotions of the audience members"

As you conclude, remember to maintain the same emotional impact you delivered in your presentation. Summarize your content in the context of how it relates to the audience members in their personal and professional lives - never turn it into a dull repetition of everything you have already discussed in your presentation.

Regardless of your topic, or whether you are appearing in front of a large audience or communicating your message to an individual, always remember that whatever information you are sharing is only useful to people if they can apply it in some way to solve problems,

94

improve their lives or to give them perspective. At all times, connect your information to them as individuals.

"Crystallize your main messages into their hearts."

Analyze your audience – 4 Different Types Of Audience

You can't fit a square peg into a round hole. Anyone who wastes their time and effort in such a fruitless task is foolish. The same is true when giving a presentation. Giving a speech that does not match up with the personality of the audience members is an exercise in futility, but a presentation that is geared to the audience will fit perfectly for all parties involved.

Always be the first one there - it will give you the opportunity to scan and analyze the audience members as they show up. There is a lot you can learn from audience analysis. Take mental notes and group the audience members into four categories of personality type then consider which category describes the majority of the audience.

The four personality types you are looking for are the following:

1. **Strong Minded** - an audience that would like you to get to the point. They will have an interest in learning but would prefer to have your message delivered in shorthand rather than drawn out. They view themselves as busy and short on time and appreciate an efficient approach to presenting.

95

2. **Analytical** - they would like the speaker to slow down and provide detailed information. Analytical types prefer to know that all your information and content is authenticated and referenced.

3. **Energetic** – they are a highly interactive and high-energy group. This group tends to move around a lot, cannot sit still, and want to have influence, be able to share their thoughts and interact throughout the presentation.

4. **Loving** –caring, supportive individuals make up this group. Their priority is to look after one another.

The Secret to Starting Your Presentation – Garbage Day

Though it is hard to measure, most experts estimate that any given person will have about 60,000 thoughts per day. With this much going on in someone's head, it is no wonder that many presenters have a hard time grabbing their audience's attention and holding onto it. Overall, presenters have an uphill battle each time they stand up to talk to an audience.

Keep in mind that when audience members walk in, they are generally thinking about their situations at work or at home; they will also be thinking about the work they will have to catch up on after the presentation is over. They are thinking of vacations, the weekend, children, clients etc. Whatever you start your presentation with will have to stop them in their tracks. Replace their present thoughts with

96

something that has an emotional impact, a thought that has greater value to them then their previous thought.

"In order to change a person's immediate thoughts,
You will need to replace those thoughts
with thoughts that are of greater value to them."

Starting your presentation strongly means connecting emotionally to your audience. The goal of your introduction should be to trigger emotions, shifting their mindset from the private thoughts that will be distracting them to what you want them to feel and think.

Start Strong

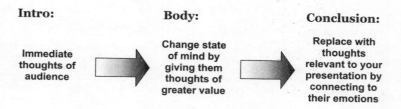

Intro:

Immediate thoughts of audience

Body:

Change state of mind by giving them thoughts of greater value

Conclusion:

Replace with thoughts relevant to your presentation by connecting to their emotions

Starting strong does not necessarily mean you have to create an impact with the first words you speak; it is a principle of changing their mind frame. You may want to start small conversations and create a little bit of interaction to loosen everyone up and then share a gripping story or message that will involve them emotionally right from the start.

The best way to shift thought process in someone is to connect with them emotionally, and the best way to do that is by relaying a message through a story that they can relate to in other aspects of their lives.

I recall a particular presentation where one of the messages I wanted to impress upon the group was awareness and patience in understanding of how others treat us. I could have gone straight to the point, laying out the message like the title chapter in a book... "Understand that they could have had a bad day, they are not really mad at you, they just have a lot on their mind and need someone to take it out on. Don't take it personally, smile, move on, don't let it ruin your day and do not pass on the negativity"
How boring is that?

You cannot run a marathon without some prep work, you don't kiss your date goodnight before dinner. Every message needs a story to connect the dots and in the case of a presentation, to connect the emotional dots. All the logical facts are great, but your audience needs to feel the message before they can visualize it.
You can help your audience feel, visualize and live your message through a poignant and relatable story that touches them in some way. The difference may sound something like this..."I would like to share a story with you about a seemingly small event that opened my eyes – I call it 'Garbage Day'.

"Replace their present thoughts with something that has an emotional impact"

I was cycling downtown with a friend when suddenly a car sped around the corner and almost hit me. I slammed on my brakes, barely managing to keep my bike upright. Although it was obvious that the driver of the car was at fault, he started yelling at me.

I put a big smile on my face and waved at him. The person I was cycling with asked me "Why did you just do that? The driver could have seriously injured you – not to mention almost damaging your bike!"

"Well," I said, "as in most neighbourhoods, we collect our garbage all week in order to dump it all on collection day. People run around full of garbage, frustration, pain, misunderstanding, stress and anger and as their 'garbage' piles up, they need a place to dump it - sometimes they dump it on you. "

So next time some one dumps their garbage on you, do not take it personally. Smile, wave and understand that it is their day to dump that garbage, wish them well, and move on.

"Your audience needs to feel the message before they can visualize it "

More importantly, do not take their garbage in, compile it in your bin and spread it to other people at work, at home with your family, your kids, friends or a cyclist on the street. The bottom line is that respected and trusted leaders do not let garbage, their own or someone else's, take over their day.

"Love the people who treat you right. And also love the people that don't"

If you provide a means for people to live your message, really experience it, they will always remember what you had to say. When the time comes that they personally experience the situation you shared with them, they will remember your story.

Ice Breakers

We all remember being in school when the teacher asks the first question. There is a long pause and silence fills the room while the seconds tick by. No one wants to speak first, and everyone is acutely aware of themselves in the group. A good teacher will know how to overcome this block of silence in order to promote a positive learning environment. A good presenter will also know how to handle this initial discomfort and apprehension in order to better reach their audience.

'Ice breakers' are a great way to influence the mindset of your audience and should be relevant to the message you are trying to convey.

By taking a bit of time to allow the audience to get to know each other you will find that when they feel comfortable with each other they will interact with you more readily.

100

Timing is crucial when introducing the use of icebreakers. Make sure there is enough time to allow for relevance of the exercise but ensure that it does not exceed a time of effectiveness, as you will lose the participants interest.

The question arises, what is effective time for an icebreaker.
First, and foremost, remember the purpose of an icebreaker - get their mindset to where you want it to be, get them to stop thinking about all the aspects of their day and start thinking about what you will be covering during the session.

If you are delivering a two day workshop, you will have time to do an icebreaker that could take approximately thirty minutes.

For a three hour workshop, your icebreaker might be about 10 minutes. Your icebreaker for a one hour keynote presentation will, more times than not, turn into a critical message that gets your audience's attention away from their daily activities and onto your topic.

The point is that icebreakers have a specific purpose for each instance. Keep that purpose in mind and you will incorporate a useful and relevant piece into your presentation.

"The purpose of an icebreaker - get their mindset to where you want it to be"

Style

The movie Toy Story tells the tale of a group of toys that belong to a young boy. Led by the practical and much loved cowboy doll Woody, the toys tentatively welcome newcomer Buzz Light Year to the room after a birthday party. Unlike the other toys, who are aware of their role and purpose in life, the new Buzz Light Year does not realize he is a toy and instead believes he is in fact a space ranger, as his box says he is.

Determined, Buzz works to prove his status. At one point, to convince any doubters, Buzz insists he can fly and attempts to prove it by flying around the room. Through a series of creative mishaps, Buzz flies off a car ramp and circles the room on a model plane hanging from the ceiling.

When he lands back on the bed, Buzz proudly boasts of his accomplishment. Woody, frustrated at Buzz's growing popularity, argues that what Buzz accomplished wasn't flying, but "falling with style."

While Woody may have been right, Buzz's flash and flair was enough to convince the other toys, earning him instant credibility and popularity, much to Woody's chagrin.

Clearly, style counts for a lot.

"No matter what we have to say, it is often how we say it that really makes a difference."

Understanding how to develop and harness your personal style can make all the difference in the success of your presentations.

Body language

Your body language is more powerful than the actual words you speak; in fact, body language is the source of 73% of all our communication.

Body language conveys two of the most valuable parts of your presentation:

1) That you care about being there and that you care about the audience.

2) That you are passionate about your topic and that you not only care about what you say, but that you adhere to the messages and values you discuss in your presentation.

Mix up your body language to make the most of this unspoken mode of communication:

- Move around
- Stand still
- Use calm hand gestures
- Switch in and out of dynamic movement

103

Your movements should have intent. Select movements and gestures that are appropriate for the tone of the story you are telling. For example, if you are telling an exciting story, use energetic gestures and move briskly. If you are telling a sad story on the other hand, then stay relatively still and use slower, more relaxed gestures.

"Your body language is more powerful than the actual words you speak"

Avoid having items in your pockets, such as loose change as you may inadvertently end up playing with it and rattling it, to the distraction of the audience.

Speakers often inadvertently exhibit annoying gestures. You will need to figure out what gestures you might be making that could distract your audience.

Make a video tape of yourself and study your gestures and movements. Once you know what you need to control and change, you can put 'memory builders' into place to rebuild your habits.

For example, if you have a habit of walking around too quickly you can strategically position some tape on the stage to remind you as you cross over it.

I once coached a speaker who had a habit of waving his arms around. A thick elastic band on his wrist was the perfect solution - it would catch his eye as his arm moved, reminding him to curtail his arm movements.

Another speaker I worked with had a habit of pointing his finger at people. He found it helpful when we encouraged him to draw a smiley face on his finger as a reminder.

> **"The principle is simple:**
> **Find the habit you want to break**
> **and create a reminder to reform it little by little"**

Voice

While email and texting have revolutionized the way people communicate, these forms of electronic communication have been criticized for their limitations. After all, it is very hard to convey emotion electronically. In normal speech, we change our tone of voice or the intensity of our speech. These small changes go a long way to communicating how we feel or what our intentions are. While these factors are difficult to produce in electronic mediums, they can be harnessed to their full potential when giving a presentation.

Modulate the tone and volume of your voice accordingly for each of the stories you are sharing. If you are discussing a profound and emotional story, stand still and keep your hands in front of you in a gentle position. Calm both your voice and movements and speak slowly and softly.

On the other hand, if you are recounting an exciting anecdote, move around, use expressive hand gestures, speak faster and modulate your voice in both high and low tones. By adjusting the tone of your voice according to the story, you will heighten the emotional impact on the audience.

Podium

Ships are designed to sail, but when their anchors are dropped, they're not going anywhere. While this immobility is important in certain situations, such as in dock or for fishing ventures, it can be harmful to try to take to the open sea with the anchor down. Therefore, a smart sailor will always lift the anchor in order to set to sea.

Just like a boat trying to set sail, a presentation needs to be unfettered in order to achieve its true potential. Because of this, it is crucial as a presenter to avoid anchoring yourself in any way, which means it is time to put away the fallback podium that has been so popular in traditional speech-giving.

The use of podiums is ill advised unless you are planning to read a speech or if you are introducing someone and reading their bio. If you are in a position where you have to read a speech, a podium is the best tool.

Standing behind a podium has several negative effects:

- **Constricts your gestures**
- **Prevents you from moving around**
- **Creates a barrier between you and your audience**
- **Hides the energy and expressiveness of your body language**

It is said that when you smile, the whole world smiles with you. This is more than a cute quote; it actually has some basis in fact. It has been proven that one smile can trigger smiles in others, instantly improving the mood in any situation.

If something as simple as a smile can make a difference, presenters should be conscious of every little thing they do. Style is developed not only in your inflection and movement, but in the way you carry yourself and your subtle connections with the audience.

Five CRITICAL elements to remember during any and every presentation:

- **Pause**
- **Relax**
- **Fun**

- **Eye Contact**
- **Smile**

The most critical moment of any presentation is the start. Most presenters want to get the ball rolling the moment they step in front of their audience, jumping right in without allowing audience to adjust their mindset and catch up.

Remember, it is okay to breathe, take a second to take in the audience and smile. This in turn slows down your heart rate, calms you and creates anticipation in the minds of the audience, allowing them to turn their focus on you.

The five elements mentioned above can be used in any combination - together, separately or one before the other. The key is to use at least one of them with every breath, every connection and message you send to your audience. Mix it up. At times, smile, at others pause more between some critical words in a sentence, or connect using eye contact with an individual. When you make strong eye contact with a relevant message to one individual in your audience, everyone will feel connected to you.

"When you smile, the whole world smiles with you"

The main principle behind using these five elements is the power they have in connecting you, your message and your audience.

Smile, relax and have fun

It is crucial that you enjoy your presentation; if you enjoy it, your audience will enjoy it. The more you smile, relax and have fun, the more you will go with the flow, appearing and feeling natural in your role as presenter.

"A smile will mask any nervousness you may feel."

Smiling and having fun has a contagious effect - you can lighten the mood of your audience with your own cheerfulness, which in turn relaxes you. Once you know your audience is enjoying themselves you will automatically relax as well because, now you have at least accomplished that!

"It is okay to breathe, take a second to take in the audience and smile"

Eye contact

Eye contact is important as it enables you to capture the attention and focus of your audience. Take care not to stare too long or you will make the recipient of this attention feel uncomfortable, and they will feel that they have been singled-out.

As a rule of thumb, cast brief glances at members of the audience. Eye contact is important because it communicates to your audience that you notice them. Many commonly make judgment that someone who does not make eye contact is a shifty character or has something to hide. If you make direct eye contact with your audience, you will enforce the fact that you believe in and stand by what you are saying and can be trusted.

The Pause

Learn the power of the pause if you want your audience to absorb what you are saying you have to give them time to digest. Use pauses during the moments where you are looking to impart the most impact to your last statement.

"Enjoy your presentation"

Learning Styles

Varieties of presentation styles

Textbook companies have made a science out of communicating content to a wide range of learners. While older textbooks employed extensive blocks of text to make their point, newer models are better geared to all types of learners. In addition to straightforward text, modern textbooks will use pictures, graphs, creative narratives, quotations, and more. Why? Because textbook companies know that people learn in different ways, and the best way to reach all learners is to appeal to all learning styles.

Unlike reading a book, your audience has one chance to listen to you - they do not have the option of re-reading a passage if they miss something or do not understand your message.

Because of the necessity for immediate audience retention, you need to keep things simple and interesting.

You also need to reach all of the audience's senses because everyone learns in a different way. Using different presentation styles will give your audience the variety they require to stay interested, and will help you reach people who learn in different ways. Use as many of the following presentation styles as possible for maximum effect: visual, emotional, logical and theoretical.

111

"Your audience has one chance to listen to you - they do not have the option of re-reading a passage"

In order to reach each person in your audience you should focus on each of the four learning styles in a sequential flow:

- Visually
- Emotionally
- Statistical
- Relevance

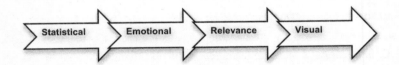

Statistical | Emotional | Relevance | Visual

Statistical

Add any facts, theory and statistical information relevant to your message to lend authenticity.

When using statistics make sure you connect them to something meaningful for audience members and their situation.

"You need to keep things simple and interesting"

Emotional

Telling a story will trigger the emotional response you require in those who learn emotionally. To elicit an emotional response, you must first ensure the story is one to which your audience can relate.

"They need to feel like the story is about them and their life situations."

I gave a presentation to a group of Psychologists and Psychiatrists and one of my messages was about the importance of staying aware of the state of mind of our patients while walking them through the process of self-awareness. The emotional response that I wanted to trigger within this group was how they have had felt in situations when others did not understand their state of mind in a particular situation.

We did this first by adjusting their state of mind, by asking them to recall a situation where someone did not understand them – a situation they most likely would encounter on a daily basis. Once they recalled a particular incident, we talked about the emotions they felt and the impact that had on them. Helping them re-live that experience allows me drive home the importance of being aware of the same situation with their clients.

Relevance

State the obvious; tell the point of your story, including what it illustrates and how that tidbit of information relates to your audience as individuals in their personal and professional life. No matter how obvious and basic the point may seem to you, you still need to mention it.

Visual

To reach them visually, display a PowerPoint picture slide that represents the story that will connect them to the message.

People do not remember content, but they can implant the visual into their minds.

"The power of the stories you share lies not in the words, but in the feelings behind them"

Story Telling –
Courage To Shed Your Armour

From elaborate wedding proposals to comic covers of hit songs, people all around the world have utilized youtube.com to become instant celebrities. Youtube.com is a video streaming site, which allows users to upload personal videos for worldwide viewing. In this medium, some people have discovered internet fame, with their performances going viral, earning thousands or millions of hits.

"State the obvious; tell the point of your story"

Why do these videos become so popular? The individuals putting them up are not professionals and most of the videos are poor quality. However, the people in them are real people. It is this authenticity that attracts people, creating a resonance that can take an average person and turn them into a viral celebrity.

This goes to show that you don't have to be an expert to open yourself up to others. Letting go of your inhibitions is hard, but

"When people see the real you, they are more likely to be engaged with what you have to say."

115

Emotion versus logic

We base every decision we make on some level of emotion directly linked to experience, which is then justified by logic. That is why, for every message you communicate, you must first open the minds of your audience with emotion and then, once they are receptive, tell them specifically the message you intend to get across.

For your audience to be receptive to what you have to say they must feel that you genuinely care about them. People do not care what you know until they know how much you care. More important than the information you impart is how you make them feel.

"One of the best ways to make your audience feel emotion is for you to display emotion."

The power of the stories you share lies not in the words, but in the feelings behind them. Allow yourself to feel the emotional weight of a story as you share it with your audience.

The best stories to draw on are your own - you will be more passionate about something you have actually experienced and as a result, your audience will relate to your message with deeper emotion.

I once spoke to a youth group. As I spent time getting to know them, it became apparent to me that each one of them had become victims of the negative circumstances they had learned to focus on.

116

What I wanted them to understand is that we are all on our own journey; our own circumstances that help us base our choices; we can choose to be victims of those circumstances, allowing them control our lives or we can tap into the potential in them and to create our own destiny.

One tactic I use to impress my point on an audience like this is to talk about people who have come from harsh circumstances similar to theirs and have gone on to accomplish great things.

"The best stories to draw on are your own"

I also balance that information with some of my own journey. I talk about some of what it I went through, how, when told I would end up in a wheel chair I refused to believe it. I share how I dreamed of one day running again and all the emotions I went through at the time. I go on to explain how facing the challenges I had come up against head on rather than becoming a victim of them also created a multitude of other joys in my life, opened so many new doors and built the lasting relationships I now hold so dear.

"Have the courage to shed your armour and share part of you to your audience."

That is a true sign of having the courage it takes to be an authentic speaker.

117

Connect Your Stories
To Different Learning Styles

In creative writing courses, many students are taught the power of appealing to all the senses. Exercises are designed to help students successfully incorporate all the senses into their storytelling in order to better reach their audiences. This varied approach not only enriches the story, but is more likely to resonate with readers.

There is more than one way to tell a story. The best way to reinforce your message is to use the presentation model to relay your message; the more you can implement visual, emotional, statistical, and relevance presentation styles, the greater the impact you will make.

At times, you might not be able to use all aspects of the model due to your environment, i.e. the absence of technology for visual aids. Whatever limitations you may encounter, remember to follow the principles of the different learning styles and connect your stories through them. If you do not have access to an LCD for slides, draw out a picture through your words and actions.

"There are more ways than one to capture your audience's imagination."

118

What Was That You Said?
Attention Span

When most people go to the grocery store, they are sure to take a list in hand. Why? Because without a list, it is likely that you will forget something that you need. For some people, even making a list isn't enough, since they manage to forget where they put it when they walk into the store.

Many researchers believe that the human attention span has actually dwindled in recent years. With TV and the internet, people are constantly distracted, making it difficult to stay focused on any one thing for a period of time. This is why after receiving explicit direction, many people still have to ask, "What was that you said?"

How often have we thought that when others are speaking?
People, in general, have short attention spans so it is important to stimulate them – do not engage in long-winded tangents.

Keep your anecdotes and messages short. Tailor your stories to stimulate emotions and never let things drag on to the point that you lose emotional immediacy. Keep your audience engaged, but also get to the point. Ensure your message is clear.

Humour –
Don't Be A Stand Up Comic

"People never forget moments of laughter."

If you can make people laugh then you will be the hit of the show but be very careful when using humor in your presentation. Comedians should be the only ones telling jokes on stage – it is their job.

Remember the sub title of this book – "Ultimate Guide To Presenting And Communicating Your Message" – it does not say "Ultimate Guide to Being a Comedian." Of course, if you are specializing in comedy as a presenter that is a different story. Otherwise, you have to be very careful how you use jokes and make fun of others.

I once observed a speaker who truly wanted to be a comedian. The first half of his presentation was amazing, he captivated the crowd, had strong stories and a relevant message. Then he said something that made the audience laugh and he took that as an invitation to continue as a comedian. His entire presentation began to change as he directed his energy toward making people laugh – as soon as he lost his authenticity and tried to be something he was not, people lost connection to him - that was the point at which his presentation began to go quickly downhill.

120

Humour in any presentation should relate to real life scenarios and is most effective when used within your stories. Use your own experiences in your stories and do not be afraid to laugh at yourself.

Humour at the expense of others will alienate your audience rather than warm them.

"People never forget moments of laughter."

Life of A Politician

Anyone in business knows that you have to put in a lot of time and effort to get new clients. Some estimates suggest that it takes up to eight conversations with a potential client before they will even agree to sit down face to face with you for a professional meeting. It takes a great deal longer to secure a sale.

This should remind us that it takes a lot of work to convince someone to believe in what you say. However, just one misstep can be enough to undermine all your hard work, no matter how thorough or convincing you may have been. This is why in business and in presentations, it is essential to always keep yourself in check or you run the risk of alienating your audience with one wrong word.

"Do not be afraid to laugh at yourself"

Take care to be politically correct in all aspects of your presentation – do not offend anyone, particularly in your choice of humor. Once you have offended someone, it will not matter how well you present - the negative impression your audience will have of you will blind them to everything positive you may do on stage.

When you are telling a story, keep the following in mind:

- **Emotion vs. Logic**
- **Connect to the learning styles of people in your audience**
- **Audience attention span**
- **Humour**
- **Political correctness**

"Once you have offended someone, it will not matter how well you present "

Is She An Experienced Motorcyclist?

Interaction

When most people are asked about their favorite sport, they usually need to have the question clarified. After all, someone's enjoyment of a sport will vary drastically depending on whether they are playing or watching. While many people may enjoy playing a round of golf, there are far fewer who will take the time to watch a golf tournament on TV. The reason why is pretty simple: doing something is often more engaging than simply watching.

Interaction with your audience creates energy and relaxes people so that they are encouraged to interact. Getting a healthy level of interaction going with the audience will have many positive effects:

- It will help audience members to stay energetic
- Prevent them from losing focus
- Create a bond between audience and presenter.
- It helps them to feel involved and enjoy themselves.

At the same time, as the presenter, you have to be careful to control your crowd. Every interaction should be relevant to everyone involved.

"Action creates emotion.
The best way to engage the mind is to get the audience to
move about. Movement creates energy within the mind as
well as the body."

During exercises, get your audience to move around or stand. Instead of letting them remain sitting in groups on their tables, get them to get up and work on a flip chart.

Engage your audience by having them respond verbally or raise their hands to even the most basic questions.

Handling questions

I remember when I was new to riding motorcycles. One day I was having a coffee with a friend I used to race with. If you drive a motorbike you know the joy the sound of engines roaring in the distance brings - that sweet sound was what we heard coming nearer as we sat on the patio.

As a handful of motor bikes raced by us my friend asked "Fred, looking at them drive by, can you tell the difference between a novice and an experienced rider?"
My reply was the most technical and complicated answer I could come up with, but his focus was more on the power of the basics.

124

He smiled back at me, "Fred, you can always tell an experienced sport bike rider because they have the ball of their foot rather than the middle of their foot on the foot pegs."

Every time I sit in on a presentation, I look for one indicator to determine the experience of a speaker - his/her ability to field questions. The art of instantly answering any question without going into too much detail and the ability to connect that answer to the entire audience is one that can only come with experience.

The best way to build this skill is through experience; the second best way to build this skill is to take the time to predict any question an audience can throw your way and know how you would answer it.
The audience will test you in order to establish your credibility. You can be a great presenter but as soon as you start dancing around questions, you become the equivalent of a typical politician in their eyes and lose their trust.

Answer questions confidently but carefully, taking care not to offend anyone.

Blunt answers can save time and have more impact, but the blunt approach is only advisable after you have built a good rapport with the audience.

Answer the questions you are able to and, if you do not know the answer, advise them you will do some research and get back to them.

If you are asked an inappropriate question or one that requires too lengthy an answer or is irrelevant to the crowd, etc., advise them that you would love to answer that but it would be more appropriate and respectful of others' time if you answered it one on one after the presentation.

Above all, respond to all questions confidently in order to inspire trust and confidence in your answers.

Making Dinner With The Kids

Focus

Stay focused when presenting and do not allow the audience interaction to spin out of your control. If the discussion becomes irrelevant to the topic or theme, you must jump in and steer it back to the topic. Also, be careful not to allow audience banter to drag on for too long.

These rules as well apply to you as the presenter:

- **Stay focused on your topic**
- **Do not run off on a tangent or stray too long from your topic**

126

You need to control every aspect of your presentation, otherwise it can move in directions that will not be in keeping with your original vision and intention.

Keeping control of the presentation is not to say there is no room for improvisation or audience participation. On the contrary, you should make your audience feel that they have freedom in the presentation and that there is flexibility for them to take it in any direction they require while upholding your responsibility to maintain control.

This reminds me of making dinner with my niece and nephew. They just want to be a part of the action - they want to experience it all and be responsible for everything with you. When kids know they are a part of the result, they are proud, appreciative and engaged. It is completely irrelevant to them that you, as the adult, still ultimately have control of what and how much goes into the recipe.

We, as adults, feel the same satisfaction when we are involved in creating something. As a presenter, once you have some experience, know your content and are comfortable with your presentation, there is no need to memorize it.

> *"Allow the audience to change the recipe*
> *of the presentation a little."*

127

Giving them some control. When they see others enjoying themselves, they will all feel the same pride and self-satisfaction knowing that they were somehow responsible for everyone's enjoyment.

Unexpected Issues

Oscar Wilde is quoted as saying, "To expect the unexpected shows a thoroughly modern intellect." This quote has endured the test of time for its simple truth. No matter how well we plan and no matter what contingencies we put in place, there will always be something we cannot account for. Whether in life, business, or a presentation, the only guarantee we have is that there are no guarantees at all.

Be aware that there will always be unexpected issues during a presentation - no matter how much foresight you have or how much you prepare.

The most important thing to keep in mind is to stay focused and do not let unexpected issues throw you off course. Laugh about it; work through it and/or around it. Your audience will follow your response to the situation. If you show stress, they will feel stressed; if you are relaxed, they will stay relaxed; if you laugh, they will laugh...

"Do not let unexpected issues throw you off your presentation."

128

Cause And Effect

Presenter		Audience
Stressed	=	Stressed
Relaxed	=	Relaxed
Laugh	=	Laugh
Energetic	=	Energetic
Presenter Emotions	=	Audience Emotions

Effective Conclusions

Ending a Presentation Effectively

During its run on NBC, the sitcom Seinfeld was a rating's powerhouse. People tuned in week after week to watch the random and often pointless antics of Jerry, George, Elaine, and Kramer. So when the show came to a close, the finale was widely watched and hotly anticipated. However, the show's offbeat conclusion ended with the four main characters in jail, and people around the world were left dissatisfied.

Endings make or break. From TV to books to movies, a bad ending can sour an otherwise enjoyable experience. The same is true for any presentation you give. The right ending can make all the difference, but a bad one can undo all the work you put in.

To conclude your presentation simply summarize your main message points – what you would like your audience to take away from this event.

- Remind them of your three key points

- With each message point, add a sentence that is relevant to their lives

130

It is not necessary or advisable to run through the entire presentation; your audience will have heard it the first time.

Besides summarizing your main points, have your audience commit to what they have gained and absorbed from the presentation. Writing creates clarity and reaffirms knowledge.

To facilitate this commitment, instruct the audience to write down the main points they have gleaned from the presentation.

"Have your audience commit to what they have gained and absorbed from the presentation"

If the size of the crowd allows, ask the audience members to share what they have written. Sharing verbally creates conviction and allows everyone to hear each person's individual interpretation of what others have learned or experienced which in turn reinforces learning and often provides inspiration.

"Writing your thoughts creates clarity in your mind. Speaking your thoughts creates conviction in your heart."

Q&A

Question and answer sessions are a great way to interact but most people do not like asking questions in a crowd. To make it easier for them, create an atmosphere where they can ask questions throughout the presentation if circumstances allow.

Leave time for Q&A but ensure you have something that can effectively fill the gap if no one has questions. I always have more content than I can possibly get through in the time allotted to ensure I will never run out of things to share.

Also, keep in mind the information from the 'Handling questions' section in the 'Interaction' segment of Module Three - if people ask questions that are inappropriate for the entire audience it is best to advise them that, out of respect for others' time, you will discuss the answer to their question privately, following the presentation.

*"I always have more content
than I can possibly get through"*

Avoiding self-promotion

I often see presenters tarnish a great presentation by ending it with heavy promotion of themselves, their books, products and future courses.

If you delivered a great presentation, then you have already done the best self-promotion possible. It is appropriate to ask the client that hired you to add a brief thirty-second plug of your products at the end of your presentation, But beyond that, limit self-promotion activities to the giveaways and handouts with which you provide to the audience.

The only time you should promote yourself strongly is if you are giving a presentation to potential clients, in order to introduce them to who you are and the services and products that you offer.

"If you delivered a great presentation, then you have already done the best self-promotion possible"

Notes

Action Plan

Write 3 Critical Messages
you want to take away from this chapter.

1. _____

_____

2. _____

_____

3. _____

_____

Post-Presentation

"The Top 5% are successful because they
follow-through,
whereas the remaining 95%
just get excited."
Fred Sarkari

Post - Presentation

Feedback

Although most great performers live for the stage, most of them grow when the lights go off. All performers--from athletes to actors to musicians--will spend time reflecting on their performances after the fact. While this reflection will certainly include self-evaluation, it also will take into account the reviews and comments from others who watched the performance.

Presentations require the same kind of scrutiny, not only from our own point of view, but from audience members as well.

There are three great reasons to ask your client and your audience for feedback:

First, seeing yourself through the eyes and experiences of others is a great way to learn what you can improve. Look for consistency in feedback, which can indicate things of which you were not aware. It will also reinforce what you are good at and how you may want to refine your style.

Second, always ask for feedback so that you can use it for future credibility. Collect a roster of testimonials for your website and publications.

Third, asking for feedback has the added benefit of demonstrating to the client or audience that you care about their experience.

> *"A great way to improve is by seeing ourselves through the eyes and experiences of others."*

Refining Your Presentation

Silver is considered a precious metal throughout the world, and it is commonly used in jewelry, flatware, decoration, and more. However, silver doesn't start out shiny and smooth. To the contrary, silver that has been freshly mined is often rough and mixed with other rocks and minerals. To produce the sleek silver that has so many practical and aesthetic uses, it must be carefully refined again and again.

Our style as presenters is no different. Most presenters start out rough around the edges, but with time and diligence, we can refine our style into something that will truly shine.

After every presentation, ask yourself two critical questions:

1. What parts of the presentation went really well?

2. What parts of the presentation need to be improved?

"Always keep refining your skills, style and content."

The best way for you to improve is to ask yourself critical questions immediately after every presentation.

You always need a starting point for improvement... and every presentation is a new starting point.

Handouts

There are two reasons to provide handouts:

First, handouts are a great way to promote your name, allowing you to circulate your name and brand throughout offices and homes.

As a service provider the handouts and brochures you give out are an extension of your business card, your name and y your brand.

Second, an extra benefit of handouts is that they are very effective at reaching people with learning styles that favor reading. Some people like to go through the information after the presentation is over; their true learning begins when they can review the information in their own time and space.

Follow-up E-mail

If you have access to e-mail addresses, a follow-up e-mail is a good way to stay fresh in the minds of clients and audience members. Remember to maintain your high level of professionalism and do not lose sight of the fact that everyone's inbox is flooded with spam - this is not your opportunity to send fifteen messages in a week. Simply advise them that if they would like a particular summary you would be glad to email it to them.

Notes

Action Plan

Write 3 Critical Messages
you want to take away from this Chapter.

1. _____

_____

2. _____

_____

3. _____

_____

Summary and Conclusion
Be Naked and Naked Again

W hen people watch a professional musician play, they are often awed by what they see. Such artistry and skill combined make for a spectacular show. However, what the audience often fails to understand, is that a performer's job is much more than giving a performance on stage. In fact, for performers who are the very best in music or sports or acting, real success is far more than natural talent. It's about practice and dedication. It's about time and effort. It's about facing your fears and overcoming them.

The same is true for presenters. The best speakers are not necessarily the ones with the most innate talent. Rather, those who excel in public speaking are the ones who have conquered their inhibitions and put themselves out there. In short, to become a presenter that can affect change and create a lasting impression, you simply have to identify your fear and just face it dead on. Once you do that, the courage to be naked gets easier and your abilities as a speaker will continue to grow.

"Those who excel in public speaking are the ones who have conquered their inhibitions and put themselves out there."

143

To summarize, the key to developing a powerful presentation is to:

- Concentrate on specific clear messages
- Tailor those messages to your clients' needs
- Build your entire presentation around those messages
- Always be aware of your audience's state of mind
- Include visual, emotional, statistical and relevant presentation methods
- Conquer your fear and build confidence by researching your topic and your audience
- Visualize success
- Practice your presentation until it flows naturally

When it comes to presentation day:

- Have your bios ready for your introduction
- Focus on your audience
- Analyze your audience and use 'ice breakers' to build rapport
- Above all, connect with your audience emotionally
- Tell stories that entertain but also get your point across
- Interact with your audience in a meaningful way
- Keep your audience engaged and guide interactions

*"You simply have to identify your fear
and just face it dead on"*

Keep your style dynamic by modulating your voice and using the power of the pause; finish on time and remember to follow up so that you retain credibility; and finally, solicit feedback and use it to refine your style so that you can continuously build on your success as a presenter.

Keeping all these principles in mind will be the key to unlocking your authenticity as a speaker. Great skill as a speaker comes with practice, and the more presentations you give, the more you will develop your own personal presentation style.

Applying the guidelines outlined in this manual and course will provide a framework for building and delivering successful presentations. Through practice, you can continue to build on this foundation and master the art of speaking with power.

Overall, while the step-by-step techniques and principles presented in this book are sound building blocks for success, it is important that you never forget the quintessential emotions that should drive any presentation. Passion and authenticity are essential. A presentation guided by these two principles can make a difference that no amount of planning or posturing can achieve.

Just think of Zal and Natasha, two children who were able to captivate an audience. Training and forethought are important, but a child-like passion will transform a presentation from informational to inspirational.

Therefore, in all you do, be true to your audience and be true to yourself. If you are, you will be surprised to discover how much courage you find to be naked again and again.

"Passion and authenticity are essential."

146

Action Plan

Write down the most critical message you want to take away from each of the Chapters. Which one has the greatest impact to you and why?

Building Your Presentation:

_____

_____

Preparation:

_____

_____

Presenting:

_____

_____

Post Presentation:

_____

_____

KEYNOTES AND SEMINARS WITH FRED SARKARI

Fred Sarkari is the president of a unique sales and personal development company that seeks to empower individuals and organizations to achieve their visions, goals and dreams.

He empowers passionate people around the world to be more effective in their professional and personal lives by creating a deeper sense of awareness.

Fred is considered an expert in human behavior. He coaches, teaches and provides management consulting services to a broad range of organizations from start ups to some of the world's largest organizations.

As a presenter, Fred's unique approach combines vision with practical application, delivering a customized and personally tailored message to each audience member. This approach provides a compelling and practical message to audiences regardless of size and translates through to the programs he creates.

Fred remains highly active in providing individuals with ongoing 1-on-1 coaching from goal setting to execution.

Fred has facilitated numerous workshops for employees of various companies including: Microsoft, Wells Fargo, BMW, Scotia Bank, Coca-Cola, Home Depot, CIBC, Royal Bank, North West Mutual Funds, Ceridian, Promotional Products Association, BMO Bank of Montreal, Genworth Financial, Hilton Hotels, Midas, Four Seasons Hotels and many more.

Fred Sarkari provides services to organizations internationally. For more information please feel free to visit www.fredsarkari.com or contact Fred Sarkari personally at fred@fredsarkari.com – 800.742.2379.

PERSONAL COACHING
WITH FRED SARKARI

The benefits of coaching are truly endless, as a coach helps you to achieve your personal desired state. The most impactful benefits are linked to our coaching process for it is customized to each individual and focuses on their specific needs. Most times we our selves are not aware of what it is that we truly need, nor are we always aware of our present situation.

Through our assessment system we will help you to become aware of your specific needs and create a strategy that would benefit you.

Fred only takes a few coaching clients at a time. Coaching with Fred is all about results and implementation.

Coaching with Fred Sarkari is completely customized for your personal needs.
Please contact fred@fredsarkari.com / 800.742.2379 for more information.

INSPIRE OUR YOUTH
Mission Statement

Building hope for the future,
in the hearts & minds of our youth.

Inspire Our Youth has one purpose; Building hope for the future, in the hearts & minds of our youth.

Leadership for Life. We believe that every individual has what it takes to achieve the life that they know they are destined to live; therefore our purpose is to create awareness of inspiration that already exists within our youth. By instilling; desire, direction, passion and most importantly purpose, they may continue to create their own belief system enabling them to lead a full and productive life.

In order to create a value based family life Inspire Our Youth not only works with our youth, but with their parents as well. As parents, we need to set the example of what defines Leadership so our children can be tomorrow's leaders. Today's youth need to develop a way of thinking that will instill lifelong values they will need in order to prosper, to fight for what is right, to fight for what they believe, to become the person they know within themselves to be no matter the obstacles they are facing.

151